P

"A stellar g
From dank
ample stash of ideas to keep any stoner inspired to take their high to new heights!"

—MELANIE MARQUIS, author of *Cookbook of Shadows*

"A wonderful book. … From spellcraft to astrology, divination, and kitchen witchcraft, this book has a way for you to involve cannabis in your practice. The variety of exercises not only keeps you learning about yourself and your craft every day, but also helps you to truly integrate magic into your everyday life. The author even includes alternatives to smoking which truly makes this book useable for everyone. … Highly recommended for all levels of magical experience."

—CHARITY L. BEDELL, author of *Container Magic*

420 Days
of
WEED
WITCHERY

About the Author

Kerri Connor is the leader of The Gathering Grove (a family-friendly, earth-based spiritual group) and has been practicing her craft for over thirty-five years. She is the author of several books, including *Spells for Tough Times*, and her writing has appeared in *Head Magazine* and several Pagan magazines. Kerri earned a BA in communications and holds a medical marijuana card in Illinois. Visit her at KerriConnor.com.

To Write to the Author

If you wish to contact the author or would like more information about this book, please write to the author in care of Llewellyn Worldwide Ltd. and we will forward your request. Both the author and the publisher appreciate hearing from you and learning of your enjoyment of this book and how it has helped you. Llewellyn Worldwide Ltd. cannot guarantee that every letter written to the author can be answered, but all will be forwarded. Please write to:

Kerri Connor
℅ Llewellyn Worldwide
2143 Wooddale Drive
Woodbury, MN 55125-2989

Please enclose a self-addressed stamped envelope for reply, or $1.00 to cover costs. If outside the U.S.A., enclose an international postal reply coupon.

Many of Llewellyn's authors have websites with additional information and resources. For more information, please visit our website at http://www.llewellyn.com.

420 Days
of
WEED
WITCHERY

Spells, Rituals & Techniques
to Enchance Your Practice

Kerri Connor

LLEWELLYN
WOODBURY, MINNESOTA

FIRST EDITION
First Printing, 2025

Cover design by Verlynda Pinckney
Interior illustrations by the Llewellyn Art Department

Llewellyn Publications is a registered trademark of Llewellyn Worldwide Ltd.

Library of Congress Cataloging-in-Publication Data (Pending)
ISBN: 978-0-7387-7758-0

Llewellyn Publications
A Division of Llewellyn Worldwide Ltd.
2143 Wooddale Drive
Woodbury, MN 55125-2989
www.llewellyn.com

Printed in the United States of America

Other Books by Keri Connor

Wake, Bake & Meditate

420 Meditations

CBD for Your Health, Mind & Spirit

Conjuring with Cannabis

Ostara

Spells for Good Times

Spells for Tough Times

DISCLAIMER

Using, distributing, growing, or selling cannabis is a federal crime and may be illegal in your state or local vicinity. It is your responsibility to understand all laws pertaining to the possession or use of cannabis. Neither the author nor the publisher is accountable for the consequences derived from the possession or use thereof. Always seek the advice of a qualified health provider regarding medical or mental health questions. This book is not a substitute for medical advice. For safety purposes, always ensure any herbs you consume are food grade and safe for consumption.

White sage is an endangered plant and sacred to Indigenous people. If you use white sage, please buy from a sustainable source that benefits Indigenous people and organizations.

CONTENTS

INTRODUCTION

I love weed, and chances are if you are reading this book, you do too.

To be a weed witch, one doesn't simply add weed here and there, sprinkled throughout their practice, and call it a day. To truly be a weed witch is to incorporate cannabis into your daily life, not only through use and experimentation, but also through research and education. The greatest spiritual connections come when you are willing to devote time and energy to them. These elements blend to bring us weed witch wisdom. Cannabis has much to teach us if we allow it, but we also have the responsibility to pay attention and learn, often seeking out more information when required. You get out of your practice what you put into it. If you only practice occasionally and are wishy-washy about it, you will only get occasional, wishy-washy results. If you want the best possible results, the work is essential. Being a witch is a way of life, not a fad.

Being any type of witch comes with certain responsibilities. These responsibilities include a respect for the natural world and the varied energies it encompasses. They also include a respect for education and history. Your responsibility as a weed witch is to learn about cannabis in its various aspects to fully honor and respect the plant, its uses, and its history. For far too long, our country has lied and spread propaganda about cannabis even though it has a rich history and is capable of diverse uses. Every day our knowledge of cannabis grows, and hopefully by the time this book is published it will have been removed from the Schedule I drug list under the Controlled Substances Act. Whether it has been or not, each month we will spend time educating ourselves on distinct aspects of cannabis, including its historical uses and current legal standing.

Most importantly, be responsible and true to yourself.

A Note About Me

I have been writing about witchcraft and Paganism since the early 2000s, and I am the leader of The Gathering Grove, an earth-based, nonprofit, spiritual organization in a small, rural, northeastern Illinois town. The Grove has been in existence since 2003, evolving, as we do, over the years. My spiritual path began when I was sixteen years old and has taken twists and turns through the world of Paganism since the mid-1980s. I practice an eclectic brand of witchcraft and Paganism.

I invite you to join me on exploring the weed witch path.

What to Expect

Throughout this book we will build, add to, or replenish your witch's cupboard. If you do not have every item listed, do not worry; you are always your most valuable tool. For those witches who like to work with a variety of ingredients, this book will also help you become well stocked with a variety of supplies.

Smoking is still the most common way to consume cannabis, though many other forms now exist. Smoking is still the fastest, purest, least processed, and most natural way to consume cannabis. When we smoke weed, we personally engage the aspects of earth, air, and fire, and we represent both water (since our bodies are mainly water!) and spirit. Nonsmokers will find alternate instructions for substituting their normal consumption method in place of lighting up. Even if you do not smoke, some spells and workings will require cannabis flower for their magical energy.

I highly recommend joining or starting a witch's supply exchange group. These are groups that when you need only a small amount of an ingredient you can request to see if anyone else has it available. Our library at The Gathering Grove allows members to access our supply of herbs, candles, jars, bottles, and other supplies.

You will also be building or adding to your Book of Shadows (BOS), and plan on plenty of journal work. Being a witch isn't only about spells and rituals; it's first and foremost about learning—learning about yourself and how to live in connection with nature and the cycles of nature no matter where you live. A witch uses natural energies to create the reality they want.

In my previous book *420 Meditations*, I began each month with a supply list and will continue that tradition here to help you easily prepare for what lies ahead for you. Do not ever feel you need to jeopardize your financial situation by buying every ingredient necessary. Find what you can, and always be sure to check with other witchy friends if you only need a small amount of an ingredient. Including online friends in your search, you never know who may drop a few thorns or a tablespoon of an herb in the mail for you.

In These Pages

You will find a total of twenty-two categories in the 366 days of the year chapter. There are chapters for special holidays, monthly full and new moons, and solar events, along with thirteen additional days of "Ways of the Weed Witch" to bring the total exercises to 420. If you happen to not like a particular day's working, or if for some reason you simply cannot do what is required that day, one of the extra thirteen can be substituted. On days when it's possible to do two workings (such as the given date and a sabbat), feel free to choose or do them both. It's your practice and entirely up to you. The categories included with a brief description are:

Cerridwen's Cauldron: You will find a new topic to research and gain knowledge about. Cerridwen's Cauldron focuses on educating the self.

Lit Literature: While evaluating books based on the monthly book topic, be sure to check details such as when the book was published and by whom. In today's world of piracy, it is easy to be taken advantage of with inferior fake products. Research is imperative to ensure you are buying a reliable source of information from a dependable broker. If a deal sounds too good to be true, it usually is. Look into book reviews: Are the majority negative? If so, it's probably a safe bet to pass on it. Add any additional titles that pique your interest to your to-be-read list.

Astrological Houses: Explore your signs in the astrological houses and document what you find in your Book of Shadows. One option is to write about how they apply to your personal journey.

Soulful Searching: These deeper meditative or journaling exercises should be performed during a trancelike or couch-locked high.

Lifted Perspective: These are exercises in seeing things from a different point of view. These exercises are best performed in a deep meditative state with a trancelike high.

Delightful Dabbling: These witchy exercises are spiced up with a bit of THC. For example, when creating spell jars, take your intended use and your own aesthetic into consideration when choosing jars, bottles, or other containers. Glass-corked vials a few inches tall can be easily transported or carried around, and they do not require a lot of ingredients to completely fill all the way. You may either blend the ingredients before placing them in the jar, or layer them one ingredient at a time, whichever you find more pleasing.

Intriguing Incantations: Learn a new chant to add to your Book of Shadows. Use these chants as a starting point to conjure up new verses.

Embracing the Elements: Element-related exercises to increase your connection with elemental energies. These are often best performed with a pleasantly focused high, not a sedative one.

Growing with the Green Man: Spiritual growth and natural energy exercises to increase your connection with different natural energies. These can be performed at whatever level of high you are comfortable with.

Tempting Talisman: You will construct a new talisman. These may be created and used while high, and each talisman contains a small pinch of cannabis.

Magical Musical Movement: These activities are to include music and movement in your practice, best performed at whatever level of high you desire.

Supernatural Senses: Research, evaluate, and work with different supernatural senses. Choose whatever state of mind works best for each exercise.

Ethereal Essences: Work with and learn about different scents and their energies while also stocking your witch's cupboard.

Reclaiming the Shadow: Shadow work exercises help to remove blockages that impede your energy flow. These exercises will require various levels of being high for meditating or journaling.

Sacred Smoke: Work with and learn about different smokable herbs while also stocking your witch's cupboard. Always ensure all herbs and plant material you smoke or consume are food grade and ethically sourced, particularly when working with sacred herbs such as white sage. If possible, grow your own herbs.

Kitchen Witchery: Enjoy a simmer pot recipe to add to your Book of Shadows.

Dank Divination: These divination exercises are best performed at whatever high you find most efficient for your divination work.

Herbal Infusions: These workings will include teas, herbal infusions, and bong water infusion recipes. You may add THC to them if you wish. Using ground decarboxylated flower is preferred in these recipes, as it is the least processed and still in its natural form. Always ensure all herbs and plant material you smoke or consume are food grade and ethically sourced.

Meditation Mojo: These meditation practices are best performed at whatever high you find most comfortable for your meditation work.

Herbal Blends: Work with and learn about smokable herbal blends and also stock your witch's cupboard. Always ensure all herbs and plant material you smoke or consume are food grade and ethically sourced.

Find Your Wild: Exercises to research local native wildlife and learn how to distinguish their energies, along with other energies in the natural environment.

Vibing: Energy- and frequency-related exercises to experiment with.

Where to Begin

You can begin this book on any day of the year but be sure to read through the Getting Started chapter for a few weed witch basics.

If you have not yet read *Conjuring with Cannabis: Spells and Rituals for the Weed Witch*, I highly recommend reading it in conjunction with your daily workings to learn more about fully incorporating cannabis into your witchcraft practice.

Welcome to your weed witch journey!

Chapter 1
GETTING STARTED

No matter what day you begin, here are a few basic bits of information to get you started on your weed witch pathway.

Magical Correspondences of Weed

Let's begin with the magical correspondences of cannabis. While it is primarily an entheogen, it also corresponds to:

- Abundance
- Binding
- Clearing negative energy
- Communication with spirits
- Death
- Healing

- Hexing
- Love
- Magical amplification
- Manifestation
- Meditation
- Prosperity
- Protection
- Sleep

Sativa will also correspond with physical and mental energy, while indica strains correspond with rest and relaxation.

The effects your weed produces are also correspondences. For example, if a specific strain makes you extra giggly, then it also corresponds with happiness and joy. Keep a running list in your Book of Shadows of strains along with their corresponding effects.

Magical Substitutions

Since hemp is a type of cannabis, using it in your workings is another way to add it to your magic that won't require you to ingest THC. You can:

- Use hemp twine when string, twine, or even ribbon are called for in your spellwork.
- Use hemp paper for spellwork or ritual work.

- Use a hemp paper journal or Book of Shadows.

- Use hemp oil for your carrier oil.

Hemp or other cannabis leaves can be used as substitutes for flower in things like jars, simmer pots, mojo bags, or talismans. You won't be including THC, but you will still be using the cannabis plant.

Astrological Chart

You will want to have a complete astrological chart prepared. Don't worry if you don't know how to; there's an app for that. I personally use Co-Star, but spend some time researching and experimenting with different apps to find one with the features best for you. Be sure it includes your full chart. Each month throughout the year, we will learn more about how the houses of the zodiac work and what effects they have on us. We learn about the zodiac because working with it adds a layer of energy to our practice. Besides, when we are high enough, we feel as if we exist among the stars. You might also know someone who specializes in birth charts and will gladly welcome your business and be able to assist you with any questions you have.

Kitchen Witch Cookery

Infusing your own cannabis products gives you the opportunity to mix in your own magic while preparing your concoctions. A weed witch should stock their kitchen with a few different THC-infused basic ingredients, if possible. Canna-butter and canna-oil are easy to make and use in recipes later. Cannabis tinctures, honey, or syrups can also easily be added to many recipes. In some states, these products are also available for purchase premade. Store-bought concentrates such as Rick Simpson or hashish oil can also be kept on hand for adding extra power to your magic.

When you mix up your own products, focus on infusing your magic along with the magic of the weed into the oil, butter, honey, or whatever it is you are working with. Making these types of products requires time where the ingredients are sitting without any active participation from you. Decarboxylating takes time. Infusing takes time. It just sits there, often for hours, while you wait for the process to finish. You probably aren't going to want to sit in a meditative state the entire time.

Instead, take time at both the beginning and the end of the process to focus on your magic. Send your intentions into the product during setup and for a few minutes into the setting period. Then, when the process is finishing, again send your magic and power into your work and the final product as you pack it up for storage.

During the setting time, you can use an intention candle in a firesafe manner, incense, or a simmer pot to keep the magic and intention going while you work on other things.

Cleansing with Cannabis Incense

Cannabis-scented incense sticks can be used to add more cannabis energy to your magical practice. Throughout this book, you will use cannabis smoke mixed with intention to cleanse, charge, and bless in your workings. If you aren't a smoker or vaper and consume your THC in other forms, incense provides an ideal smoke substitute.

Before filling jars, vials, boxes, or other types of vessels, use the smoke of a lit cannabis stick to cleanse them. The stick can easily fit inside the vials and bottles to do the work.

When using this method, say:

I cleanse and bless with this smoke,
Its magical essence I do invoke.

Save your cannabis incense ash to make black salt or to use in place of cannabis ash if you don't smoke.

Moon Water

Moon water is a staple in a witch's cupboard, and if you are a bong smoker, you can use it in place of regular water for your spiritual or witchy work.

Moon water is water blessed and charged by the energies of the moon. Moon water is usually made during the full moon, but you can also capture and contain the energies of other lunar events. A new moon, blue moon, black moon, or lunar eclipse all resonate their own specific energy. Stock a variety of moon waters in your cupboard.

To make moon water, fill a translucent (preferably glass) vessel with clean, filtered water. You can use water from a natural source such as a lake or river, but be sure to filter it so nothing ends up growing in it. If the temperature is below freezing, remember to allow space for the water to expand as it freezes so the glass won't crack or explode.

Place the vessel either outside under the moon's light or in a window where the moonlight will reach it. Say:

> *Blessed by the moon up above,*
> *Infuse this water with energies of*
> *The moon's power to work for me.*
> *Store its essence, so mote it be.*

You can then charge your moon water even further with crystals, stones, or herbs to incorporate them and their energies into your practice. Customize your water for what you need.

I have a transparent glass ritual water bottle that has two separate compartments. The top section holds the water, while the separate bottom compartment may hold crystals, stones, or even herbs, and they will remain dry while still being in close proximity to the water.

Another way to charge your moon water is to pour it into a jar, pitcher, bottle, or other vessel that is then placed inside of a bowl filled with crystals, stones, chips, or herbs. Look at thrift stores for interesting, cool pieces to transform into magical tools.

Whatever you choose to use, we will refer to this as your "water charger" for the rest of this book.

Book of Shadows Blessing

Your Book of Shadows is the collection of knowledge you obtain and the experiences you encounter along your path throughout your Craft.

Bless it under a new moon for new beginnings. Hold the book under the dark of the new moon or close to your heart and say:

In this book, I write my journey,
Knowledge gained, experiences worthy.
This is the path I walk through life,
Learned through trial: success and strife.
Protect it, keep its secrets safe for me;
Blessed for use by this weed witch, so mote it be.

Blow your smoke or waft cannabis incense smoke all around it to bless it.

Journal Blessing

Whether you use one journal or several, bless each one before its use. You may do this under a new moon for new beginnings if you don't mind waiting for one.

Hold the journal either under the darkness of the new moon or close to your heart and say:

> *In this journal I keep my thoughts,*
> *Goals, shadow work, hopes, and doubts.*
> *Protect it, keep its secrets safe for me;*
> *Blessed by the smoke of cannabis, so mote it be.*

Take a hit and blow your smoke all around your journal or use the smoke from cannabis incense to bless it.

Ash Collection Container Blessing

Ash is the combination of earth, fire, and air. Cannabis ash emptied and saved from bowls (or from smoking joints or blunts) has magical uses. It can be used in spell jars, in talismans, to create black salt, and for other purposes. Dedicate a spill-proof container to collect and store your "cannabash."

Cleanse your container with either your own smoke or the smoke from cannabis incense. Bless it under a new moon by saying:

> *With each inhalation I perform,*
> *Air, earth, fire—energy transform.*

The phoenix arises from the ash,
Magic contained in my burnt grass.
In this [jar, box, or container], this power I pour.
Bless its workings evermore.

Continually add to (and use) your ashes as necessary. Save the ash from your cannabis incense too.

Cannabis Storage Blessing

Witches love jars, boxes, chests, trunks, and other fun, useful storage containers. It's a witch thing.

Choose and dedicate boxes or other containers to store and charge your weed or other cannabis products in. I use several wooden boxes (including repurposed, refinished jewelry boxes), small chests, and antique crystal or glass sugar bowls with lids. A medium-size chest can hold jars of flower, bags of edibles, bottles of tinctures, or other products while keeping them in their original packaging.

Dedicate specific boxes or bowls to specific purposes. For example, I have one small wooden box with a triple moon engraving on the lid. This box holds a dream blend premixed and charged with a moonstone so it is always ready for me to use. I have a crystal sugar bowl that holds my divination blend while it's being charged with amethyst, clear quartz, and obsidian.

Charge your herbs and cannabis by placing your crystals and stones into a small bag and adding it to your container.

Bless your containers under the full moon by saying:

Magical tool for me to use,
Protect what I introduce.
When filled with ingredients I provide,
Magic will be harvested and stored inside.

You will use these containers throughout the year to charge your weed and other products with specific crystals and stones.

These basics will help you get started on your daily practice.

Chapter 2
366 DAILY SPELLS, RITUALS, AND TECHNIQUES

In this chapter, you'll find an activity for every day of the year. You don't need to get high every day, but these exercises are available for your use when you'd like to. Feel free to substitute any day's activity with one from chapters 3–6.

January

It's the beginning of a new calendar year, and ads will be bombarding you with ways to spend your money on tons of products to meet your New Year's resolutions. Tune out the ads and instead invest in yourself. Focus on developing and incorporating new magical methods to build your own success.

January Supply List

January 2

5 × 5-inch square piece of gold material

Small piece of dried elder (leaves, bark, or wood)
(Use gloves to handle due to toxicity issues.)

Small piece of dried oak (leaves, bark, or wood)

Amethyst stone or a few chips

Essential oil, dried herb, or resin: bergamot, vervain,
frankincense, myrrh, patchouli, sandalwood

Pinch of dried cannabis flower

Small Wheel of Fortune tarot card image or sketch

6 inches of thin purple ribbon

January 5

Small green candle (birthday, spell, or chime size)

Lighter

January 8

Glass jar with lid or corked vial

Dried: angelica, basil, chamomile, clover, lemon
balm, cannabis (you may use dried leaves as a
substitute)

Bloodstone

Aventurine chips

Small piece of paper (optional)

Writing instrument (optional)

Enough silver string to wrap around the top and tie on a charm of your choice

Charm that represents success to you

January 10

Cannabis incense (optional for nonsmokers)

January 14

Cannabis incense (optional for nonsmokers)

January 15

Glass jar with lid or corked vial

Aquamarine chips

Dried: comfrey, morning glory, mugwort, cannabis

Dandelion (fluff if available; if not, dried leaves)

Small piece of paper (optional)

Writing instrument (optional)

Orange sealing wax

Enough brown string to wrap around the top and tie on a charm of your choice

Charm that represents safe travel to you

January 16

Dried motherwort

January 17

Vanilla extract

Dried or fresh: bergamot, blue vervain, chamomile buds, lemon balm, sweet woodruff, yarrow, cannabis

January 19

Clove

January 20

Clove

January 24

Cannabis incense (optional for nonsmokers)

January 26

Dried: chamomile, lemon balm, blue vervain

Ground cloves

January 30

Clear quartz

JANUARY 1
LIT LITERATURE

Before delving into history, investigate today's modern approach to beginner Paganism. Information changes over the years, and while books written fifty years ago on Paganism are still important, we consistently learn new information, including proving old theories to be incorrect. Begin your journey by learning about today's views on beginner Paganism. Look for a title that was published within the past ten years, the more recent the better. You will explore more historical books later.

No matter where you shop for books, use the keywords "modern beginner Paganism" in your search to find titles of interest.

JANUARY 2
TEMPTING TALISMAN

Since January is often a time of setting goals and resolutions, back up your mundane workings with a bit of a magical push from this success talisman. As you create your talisman, focus on what success looks like for *you*. What do you need to have accomplished to see yourself as successful? Bring these things to mind as if they are already complete, your success is already assured. You *are* successful. Pour this energy into your talisman as you give it life.

Try to use a mix of oils and dried ingredients if available to you. Use a pinch of dried ingredients and a drop or two of oils. Be careful not to oversaturate your dry ingredients with oil, as it will become quite messy.

You will need:

- 5 × 5-inch square piece of gold material
- Small piece of dried elder (leaves, bark, or wood) (Use gloves to handle due to toxicity issues.)
- Small piece of dried oak (leaves, bark, or wood)
- Amethyst stone or a few chips
- Bergamot (essential oil, dried herb, or resin)
- Vervain (essential oil, dried herb, or resin)

- Frankincense (essential oil, dried herb, or resin)
- Myrrh (essential oil, dried herb, or resin)
- Patchouli (essential oil, dried herb, or resin)
- Sandalwood (essential oil, dried herb, or resin)
- Pinch of dried cannabis flower
- Small Wheel of Fortune tarot card image or sketch (make it no more than 1 × 2 inches; do an internet image search if you need inspiration)
- 6 inches of thin purple ribbon

Smoke your weed (or use another consumption method, allowing time for edibles to take effect) while you assemble your ingredients and create this talisman. If you have room to work at your altar, do so, or create another sacred space where you have room and are comfortable.

Lay the gold square on your altar or other stable location. Begin with the largest ingredients you are working with—stones or wood chips are usually biggest. Add these to the center of the material.

Next, add any smaller dried herbs (including your flower), resins, or chips. Top these off with one to two drops of any essential oils you use. Drip them onto a dried herb or piece of wood so they soak into those instead of just the material. Place the small Wheel of Fortune image on top.

Remember to focus on your vision of success as you work. Imagine the energy of yourself being successful. What does it feel like? Is it filled with pride and gratitude? What emotions does success evoke for you? Pour those feelings and energies into your talisman.

When you are done filling it, bunch the material up into a pouch and wrap the purple ribbon around the neck three times before knotting it off. As you wrap and tie the ribbon, say:

> *The Wheel of Fortune—its power I see.*
> *Success I call to reside in me.*
> *These energies here I do contain,*
> *Tie success to my name.*
> *What I command, make it be.*

Trim off any extra ribbon. Carry this talisman with you when you want to reharness and utilize these energies for success.

JANUARY 3
SOULFUL SEARCHING

Smoke your weed (or use another consumption method, allowing time for edibles to take effect). Begin the new year with this journaling exercise, exploring what success means to you. How do you personally define success? What specific examples can you give? Has your vision of success changed over the years, and if so, how? How important is the concept of success to you? Where have you had the most success in your life? In what ways have you found success elusive?

JANUARY 4
ASTROLOGICAL HOUSES

Research the meaning of the astrological first house and explore the role it plays in your life within your own chart. The first house represents the self and your personality. This is where your ascendant resides. Record the information you learn and how it relates to your sign and yourself in your Book of Shadows or a journal.

JANUARY 5
DELIGHTFUL DABBLING

Work a little success candle magic with this quick and easy spell.

You will need:

- Small green candle (birthday, spell, or chime size)
- Lighter

Hit your high. Then, before lighting the candle, hold it in both of your hands. Feel the texture of the candle and how the warmth of your hands affects it. Imagine your desire for success moving through your body, congregating, collecting, flowing into your arms, traveling to your hands, through your fingers, and onto the surface wax of the candle. Place the candle at the center of your altar or in another location in a fireproof dish and light in.

As you focus on the flame of the candle, visualize what success looks like for you. Allow the candle to burn almost all the way out while you continue visualizing your success. Before the candle extinguishes itself, take another hit and say:

> *So toke it be,*
> *So mote it be,*
> *Bring the success I desire to me.*

Take one more hit (or deep, centered, intention-filled breath if you do not smoke or vape) and use your exhalation to extinguish the candle flame, sending your energies to the universe.

JANUARY 6
CERRIDWEN'S CAULDRON

This month, research or review some foundational information. Focus on the separate phases of the moon and what the names of each monthly full moon are, along with their correspondences. Add this information to both your calendar and your Book of Shadows.

If you can, experiment with different strains or products to find which ones you associate with the moon phases and each full moon. Document this information too. New strains and products become available all the time, so keep a running list in your BOS.

JANUARY 7
INTRIGUING INCANTATIONS

Incantations and chants don't have to be reserved only for formal spellwork. Use them throughout the day while you are doing other things (like smoking your weed!) to send some magical zaps into the universe. Words have power. Use yours.

Use this incantation to draw success to you and your life.

What I want and what I need,
Will always find its way to me.

In the air, energies spin.
In the end, I always win.

Chant or sing it to yourself or aloud to set your winning attitude.

JANUARY 8
DELIGHTFUL DABBLING

Harness the powers of success and store them for your use in this spell jar. You'll need enough ingredients to fill your chosen jar or vessel.

You will need:

- Glass jar with lid or corked vial
- Angelica (dried)
- Basil (dried)
- Chamomile (dried)
- Clover (dried)
- Lemon balm (dried)
- Cannabis (dried) (you may use dried leaves as a substitute)
- Bloodstone
- Aventurine chips

- Small piece of paper (optional)
- Writing instrument (optional)
- Enough silver string to wrap around the top and tie on a charm of your choice
- Charm that represents success to you

Smoke your weed (or use another consumption method, allowing time for edibles to take effect). Place each ingredient into your chosen jar (or mix them in a bowl and then transfer them to your jar), focusing on each one's energy along with your intention.

As you work with each ingredient, say:

I call upon the power of [ingredient name],
Bring to me the energy of success.

If you are working on a specific project, write a manifestation statement of success on a piece of paper and place it in the jar.

Take a hit (or deep, centered, intention-filled breath if you do not smoke or vape) and use your exhalation to gently blow your hopes and objectives into your jar.

Seal the top of the jar. Wrap the silver string around the jar top and attach the charm. When finished, say:

In this vessel,
Combine together,

Keep your power here.
In this vessel,
Combine together,
Keep the magic near.

You may either carry your jar with you when you need its energy or set it in a place related to what success you need, for example on a desk or office shelf where it is easy to see and access.

JANUARY 9
FIND YOUR WILD

Find a place to take a nature break today and seek out the natural energies of winter. After you get high, spend at least fifteen minutes outside, preferably in a location with as few other people and distractions as possible. Close your eyes and tune out all manufactured energies around you. Eliminate human-caused sounds and scents. Allow yourself several minutes to adjust to the energies around you and shuffle through them, marking those you can for ignoring. What natural forces can you detect? What do you hear? What do you smell? What do you feel in the air?

JANUARY 10
EMBRACING THE ELEMENTS

Fire is an essential component in cannabis consumption, no matter how you use it. It is heat that turns THCA into THC, burning off the extra acid. The heating of THC is also what allows us to use it to obtain a high. In all forms of cannabis, whether extracts, flower, or edibles, there is at one point a heating process that helps to bring us to our high. When we smoke cannabis, we experience the use of heat firsthand through fire.

Light your cannabis in whichever manner you prefer to smoke it and pay close attention to the process. If you do not smoke, use a cannabis-scented incense stick, and focus as you light it. Listen to the fire as it burns the plant material. Smell the smoke. Watch the red embers as they brighten and then fade. This is the energy of fire. It is both giving and destructive. Fire helps to give cannabis the power to help you. Meditate on the power of fire in connection to your use of it with cannabis.

JANUARY 11
GROWING WITH THE GREEN MAN

While the dead of winter may not seem like the time to be growing with the Green Man, all life cycles have a period of rest, and there is much to be learned within this rest too. During this time of rest, our actions turn more inward than outward.

Get high and take a meditative journey through the rest of the natural world. Think about the roots under the ground—resting, storing energy to be able to resume growth in the spring. Animals that hibernate also rest, storing energy to give birth to their young in the spring. Meditate on what resting and storing energy entails for you. Do not think about any of your future plans; focus only on what this rest means for you. After your meditation, journal about your experience.

JANUARY 12
SUPERNATURAL SENSES

Objective clairvoyance is the skill of seeing entities physically with your eyes. It is possible we are born with this ability and lose it or shut it off as we get older. "Invisible friends" may be explained by the ability to see spirits. Losing this skill may be a result of adults telling children an imaginary friend isn't real. As we grow and our brains and awareness develop more, the idea of seeing entities others do not also becomes quite scary, and so people learn to shut it down. Seeing things that others do not can make a person feel like they are going crazy. These negative feelings can lead to suppression of this and other psychic senses.

Weed may be beneficial for some to help regain lost skills. Because it helps to lower your walls and connect with different energies, it can help boost or amplify your skills, even if you are new to the practice or unaware of what your skill level is.

Did you have imaginary friends? What do you recall about those friends? What do you remember about those friends "disappearing"? What is your experience with objective clairvoyance? Are you a current practitioner? Document this in your BOS as your baseline, keeping space available to update in the future.

Use this quick exercise to practice your skills. Try it both with and without the aid of THC to compare the difference.

Focus on an object across the room or about ten to twelve feet away from you. Take notice of what you see in your peripheral vision, but keep your focus on the object. This peripheral field is often where clairvoyant visions appear. Open yourself to seeing what you can in this liminal field of vision. Occasionally choose another object, one closer, and focus on it instead, adjusting the liminal space around you. When you can, perform these exercises outside for more connection with the natural world.

If you are interested in this, be sure to add this topic to your research list to gather more information.

JANUARY 13
RECLAIMING THE SHADOW

Slip into a high you are comfortable using for your shadow work to perform this journaling exercise.

While we aim for success, we do accumulate failures along the way. How we deal with failure may involve aspects of our shadow selves. Often, we beat ourselves up and kick ourselves when we are down for not succeeding in the way we wish. What shortcomings or failures have you experienced but have not forgiven yourself for? Focus on how you can forgive yourself now. Allow yourself to not be perfect and to learn from your mistakes. What did your failings teach you? Write about your experiences.

JANUARY 14
DANK DIVINATION

Begin your year discovering what is to come with this twelve-month preview tarot or oracle reading.

Smoke a bowl, open your mind, and as you shuffle your tarot or oracle deck, blow smoke across your cards. (If you do not smoke or vape, you may use the smoke of cannabis-scented incense and get high with another consumption method.) Connect with your higher self or power and lay out twelve cards. Focus on each month as you shuffle and lay out a card, refocusing and reshuffling for each month.

What messages do the cards have for you? Document your drawn cards and their meanings in your journal. Explore your reading in meditation.

JANUARY 15
DELIGHTFUL DABBLING

Create a protective bubble around you with this safe-travel spell jar.

You will need:

- Glass jar with lid or corked vial
- Aquamarine chips

- Comfrey (dried)
- Morning glory (dried)
- Mugwort (dried)
- Pinch of cannabis (dried)
- Dandelion (fluff if available; if not, dried leaves)
- Small piece of paper (optional)
- Writing instrument (optional)
- Orange sealing wax
- Enough brown string to wrap around the top and tie on a charm of your choice
- Charm that represents safe travel to you

Smoke your weed (or use another consumption method, allowing time for edibles to take effect). Place each ingredient into your chosen jar (or mix them in a bowl and then transfer them to your jar), focusing on each one's energy along with your intention. Visualize a protective bubble being created around you as you build and bless your jar.

As you work with each ingredient, say:

I call upon the energies of [ingredient name],
Protect me on my travels.

If you are traveling to a specific destination, write it on a piece of paper and place it in the jar.

Take a hit (or deep, centered, intention-filled breath if you do not smoke or vape) and use your exhalation to gently blow your hopes and objectives into your jar.

Close the top of the jar and cover it with the melted sealing wax. Wrap the brown string around the jar top and attach the charm. When finished, say:

> *In this vessel,*
> *Combine together,*
> *My safety always clear.*
> *In this vessel,*
> *Combine together,*
> *Protect me here and there.*

When you travel, carry your jar or vial with you in a purse, pocket, briefcase, or suitcase, or place it in your car.

JANUARY 16
SACRED SMOKE

While motherwort has many medicinal uses, it can also be smoked for a mild high. Motherwort helps ease anxiety and release stress while promoting self-love and peace. When combined with an indica strain, it boosts the calming traits of both.

Introduce yourself to motherwort by using it on its own several times first, exploring it with all your senses. How does it look? Smell? Feel? Taste? You may either smoke it or make a tealike infusion by soaking the leaves in hot water to drink.

How does it affect you? What do you feel when using it? How long does it take to feel the effects? How long do the effects last? Evaluate and learn how motherwort works with your body and mind. Document this information in your Book of Shadows.

Once you become familiar with this herb, combine it with cannabis and again explore the effects, being sure to document your results. This herb can be combined with others to create blends.

JANUARY 17
KITCHEN WITCHERY

Begin this simmer pot spell for success in the morning by combining the ingredients in a pot of water. Allow the pot to simmer throughout the day to disperse the energy throughout your home.

You will need:

- 1 teaspoon vanilla extract
- 2 tablespoons bergamot (dried or fresh)
- 1 teaspoon blue vervain (dried or fresh)

- 1 tablespoon chamomile buds (dried or fresh)
- 2 tablespoons lemon balm (dried or fresh)
- 1 tablespoon sweet woodruff (dried or fresh)
- 1 teaspoon yarrow (dried or fresh)
- Pinch of cannabis (dried or fresh)

As you prepare the ingredients and add them to the pot, pour intention into your work. Focus on drawing success into your life.

Keep the pot on a low flame on a back burner. Stir the pot nine times clockwise once every hour throughout the day.

Each time you stir the pot, say:

Fire, water, earth, and air,
My magic has a little flare.
Fruits from the earth simmer here.
Success I command to appear.

Add more water as needed to replenish what has evaporated. At the end of the day, pour the remains outside on the ground near a tree or under a bush. Return the plant material to the earth it came from. Add this recipe to your BOS and record your own experience with it.

JANUARY 18
DELIGHTFUL DABBLING

While counting backward from one hundred may sound like an easy exercise, it is one of extreme focus. It may take a lot of practice to be able to perform, particularly when stoned, but this makes it more interesting. You may even want to have a partner nearby, listening as you attempt to count aloud and see how far you can make it without your mind wandering off in other directions. Don't feel bad if it takes a lot of practice. You may even want to try it completely sober several times before adding getting high into the mix.

Take your time working on it and see how far you can go. Continue to practice obtaining better focus and control.

JANUARY 19
ETHEREAL ESSENCES

Research the different correspondences and uses associated with cloves and add a small supply to your witch's cupboard. Whole cloves can be ground later for use. Clove oil is also great to have on hand for medicinal purposes, particularly for its antibacterial and antifungal properties, and its ability to ease tooth pain. Be sure to add to a carrier oil if using on your skin. Add the information you find to your BOS.

Dried clove can be smoked, combined with cannabis, or made into a tea. Meet the essence of clove in the following meditative practice.

Get into an elevated high and comfortable position with a small container of cloves or bottle of clove oil placed in front of you.

Close your eyes and take several deep breaths. Allow your mind to settle and focus. When you are ready, pick up the clove or clove oil and hold it about four inches away from your nose. (Begin further away if using an oil and slowly move it closer if necessary.) Inhale the scent, breathing deeply. If it's not too overpowering for you, move the clove or oil closer. Some people have sensitivities, so don't feel you have to move it directly under your nose. Oils are very potent and should not be moved as closely.

How does this scent make you feel? Is it pleasing? Irritating? Relaxing? Exciting? Powerful? Meditate on the feelings it evokes in you.

Journal about your experience. If you feel the need to clear the scent from your nose, sniff coffee beans or grounds to help neutralize the scent.

JANUARY 20
HERBAL INFUSIONS

Cloves have several medicinal benefits, including being antibacterial and anti-inflammatory. Cloves are also used magically for many purposes, including protection, attraction, courage, mental stimulation, and more.

Boil three whole cloves for nine minutes to make a clove infusion to drink. Meet the essence of a clove infusion with the following meditative practice.

Get into an elevated high and comfortable position with a cup of your clove infusion in front of you.

Close your eyes and take several deep breaths. Allow your mind to settle and focus. When you are ready, pick up the infusion and hold it about six inches away from your nose. Inhale the scent, breathing deeply. Take a moment to appreciate the scent. Next, take a slow, long sip, letting the liquid hit all areas of your tongue. Focus on the taste and how it feels.

How does this infusion make you feel? What are your thoughts on the taste? Meditate on the feelings it evokes in you, and document this information in your Book of Shadows.

JANUARY 21
VIBING

When you are high, you are better able to detect and connect with energies around you. Try out this energy exercise both before getting high and then again after you are to see what differences you can feel.

Sit in a comfortable position, relaxing the rest of the body. Place your hands in front of you, palms facing each other. Visualize sending energy into the palms of your hands. Begin rubbing your hands together rapidly, building up warmth and more energy. Continue for about thirty seconds and then gently let your hands fall apart, palms still facing each other but about six inches apart. What do you detect in the area between your hands?

Slowly move your hands closer together. Can you feel the energy shift? Move your hands further apart and closer together several times. What do you experience?

Repeat several times (both not high and high) to see how much more you can feel and detect each time. Journal about your experiences.

JANUARY 22
SOULFUL SEARCHING

Lower your walls and step into your higher self by achieving a deep meditative high. Keep the thought "Who am I?" in the back of your mind, but allow your mind to wander off where it wants to. Your higher self will direct you to what you are ready for. What do you see? What does your mind reveal to you about yourself? Journal about your journey and what you learn.

JANUARY 23
RECLAIMING THE SHADOW

Since we are focusing on success this month, reevaluate some of your life goals—not just what you want to accomplish this year, but things you want to accomplish in your life overall. Which of your goals are realistic? Which of your goals might not be very realistic? What makes your goals achievable or unachievable? What is holding you back or blocking your way? How can you overcome obstacles in your path? Use your high to brainstorm either through meditation, journaling, or both.

JANUARY 24
DANK DIVINATION

Charge your divination tools with Mary Jane magic. Whatever tools you use—pendulum, tarot cards, oracle decks, crystal ball, or scrying mirror—cleanse and bless them with smoke from your weed.

The easiest, most effective way is through a bong hit, blowing the smoke over and around your tools. Of course, you can also use a pipe or joint, or even burn a small amount of flower in a fireproof container and pass the tools through the smoke. (Cannabis-scented incense is also an alternative.) Visualize the smoke charging your divination device with the plant magic of cannabis. You can use this cleansing before each use to help build the connection between yourself, your weed, and your divination method.

JANUARY 25
MEDITATION MOJO

The state of the mind during meditation is the basis for working magic. When we can see things in our minds, we can make them real in our lives. Meditation has many known benefits for the mind, but that doesn't mean we have discovered all the answers to what our minds in a meditative state are fully capable of. We do know meditation changes the mind, and the energies derived from meditation help change our realities.

Get high and meditate on this very concept. What we meditate on, we can make real. What successes have you had? What have you manifested into your life through meditation? Where have you experienced failures or setbacks in your manifestations? Brainstorm innovative approaches. Journal about your experience. Keep track of your successful meditation manifestations in your Book of Shadows.

JANUARY 26
HERBAL BLENDS

Use this blend to accompany your success-themed spellwork. You may either add it to your cannabis to smoke or make a tea infusion.

You will need:

- Chamomile (dried)
- Lemon balm (dried)
- Blue vervain (dried)
- Ground cloves

Combine equal parts of all the herbs. Use a grinder and blend together. Add a sprinkle of ground cloves, and then add to your weed in a one-to-one ratio.

Focus on the success you are seeking as you combine and grind your herbs together, infusing the blend with your intention and energy.

Add this recipe, how it feels, and your results to your Book of Shadows. If you desire, adjust ratios for flavor.

JANUARY 27
FIND YOUR WILD

Connect to the night sky with a good high. You do not have to see the stars with your physical eyes if you picture them in your mind's eye. A galaxy map can show you where you are in relation to constellations and the moon to help you get your bearings and give you images to visualize.

Stand outside in the dark with your face to the sky. Either stare into space, taking in everything you can see—the stars, the moon, even satellites and airplanes cutting across the sky—or if it is too cloudy or your view is disrupted by light pollution, picture them in your mind. The energies of air and celestial bodies are all around you. How do these energies feel to you? How do you differentiate them from one another? How can you best utilize them? Add this information to your Book of Shadows.

This exercise will be done monthly throughout the year because as the night sky changes, the energies you feel will also change.

JANUARY 28
MAGICAL MUSICAL MOVEMENT

Start a playlist of success-themed songs. This playlist can be used when you want to raise energy for spellwork, to help focus your attention on success, or simply as background music while you do any type of success prep or spellwork.

Try out your playlist by choosing a few songs to move to in whatever type of dance you like to raise energy. Get yourself to a good, elevated, happy high (sativa or a hybrid recommended).

Focus on what extreme success would look like to you: The international adoration of Taylor Swift? The athleticism of LeBron James? The knowledge of Stephen Hawking? Combine them all together if you wish. Brainstorm in a meditative manner during your happy high on what ultimate success in your life would look like. The sky is the limit. Feel the confidence of success. Visualize the qualities of success you want to harness. Raise your energy and release it into the universe to bring these qualities to you.

JANUARY 29
LIFTED PERSPECTIVE

Weed is incredibly beneficial in helping us see events, relationships, and other incidents from a different point of view. As your walls lower and your mind elevates, it becomes easier to perceive the environment around you with your higher self. This higher self can examine and evaluate what you encounter on an unbiased level. This higher self holds an impartial opinion on your actions.

Get into a comfortable meditative position and an elevated high. Visualize your body in your mind's eye in your meditative position. You can do this by stepping back and away from yourself. *Look* at what you are doing. *See* in your mind how your body is positioned. See what you are wearing, how your hair is styled. Observe yourself in this meditative manner and make mental notes of what you see. Practicing this will help you to learn how to slip more quickly into your objective higher self.

JANUARY 30
DELIGHTFUL DABBLING

Cleanse weed with clear quartz to take away any negative vibes it may have picked up during production. A trimmer having a difficult day could put negative energy into your weed. Wipe it away with a quartz crystal.

For a quick cleansing, hold your weed (or other cannabis product) in your nondominant hand with your quartz crystal in your dominant hand. Move the crystal all over and around the weed and say:

> *Cleanse and clear,*
> *Cleanse and clear,*
> *Any negativity,*
> *Disappear.*

If you dedicate a small box, chest, or other type of container for all your cannabis products, you can charge the contents by placing a quartz crystal inside.

JANUARY 31
SOULFUL SEARCHING

Settle into a comfortable high, reflect over the past month, and journal about your growth. What successes did you find? Where did you experience shortcomings or failures? How did these experiences add to your magical practices or spirituality?

February

You've heard the saying "It is always darkest before dawn." February, while the shortest month, is the last, often darkest, stretch before spring and the return of more daylight hours. Following along with the energies of the natural world, our workings are focused inward. It is the ideal time to work on a variety of types of healing: emotional, spiritual, mental, and even physical. This month, focus on your healing in whichever aspects you need.

February Supply List
February 2

    5 × 5-inch square piece of green material

    Hematite stone or a few chips

    Small piece of dried apple (leaves, bark, wood, or fruit)

Essential oil, dried herb, or resin: dragon's blood, peppermint, pine, witch hazel

Cannabis flower (dried)

6 inches of thin brown ribbon

Cannabis incense (optional for nonsmokers)

February 5

Small red candle (birthday, spell, or chime size)

Lighter

Cannabis incense (optional for nonsmokers)

February 11

Cannabis incense (optional for nonsmokers)

February 14

Mirror

Pink candle

Rosebuds (dried)

Lighter

February 16

Holy basil

February 17

Apple

Orange

Cloves

Cinnamon sticks

Pine needles

Allspice

Ginger

Coriander

Thyme

White ground pepper

Cannabis

February 18

Cannabis incense (optional for nonsmokers)

February 19

Sandalwood

February 20

Elderberries (thoroughly cooked to remove toxicity)

Crushed allspice

Ground cinnamon

Whole cloves

February 24

Dried: mugwort and cannabis

February 26

Dried: lavender buds, sacred lotus petals, rose petals

February 29

Mugwort

FEBRUARY 1
LIT LITERATURE

Cannabis has had a tumultuous history in America, and plenty of it has been covered up, particularly in the last one hundred years. Now that we can look back and more clearly see what has happened in the past and we have easier access to information, the previous propaganda doesn't hold up under scrutiny. Broaden your knowledge this month by focusing on the true history of cannabis (and hemp) in the United States.

No matter where you shop for books, use the keywords "cannabis history United States" in your search to find titles of interest. Add any additional titles that pique your interest to your to-be-read list.

FEBRUARY 2
TEMPTING TALISMAN

While you work on creating this healing talisman, focus on what healing looks like for *you*. What do you need to have accomplished to see yourself as healed? What type of healing do you need? Bring these things to mind as if you are already healed in whatever aspect it is. You *are* healed. Pour this energy into your talisman as you give it life.

Try to use a mix of oils and dried ingredients if available to you. Use a pinch of dried ingredients and a drop or two of oils.

You will need:

- 5 × 5-inch square piece of green material
- Hematite stone or a few chips
- Small piece of dried apple (leaves, bark, wood, or fruit)
- Dragon's blood (essential oil, dried herb, or resin)
- Peppermint (essential oil, dried herb, or resin)
- Pine (essential oil, dried herb, or resin)
- Witch hazel (essential oil, dried herb, or resin)

- Cannabis flower (dried)
- 6 inches of thin brown ribbon
- Cannabis incense (optional for nonsmokers)

Smoke your weed (or use another consumption method, allowing time for edibles to take effect) while you assemble your ingredients and create this talisman. If you have room to work at your altar, do so, or create another sacred space where you have room and are comfortable.

Lay the green square on your altar or other stable location. Begin with the largest ingredients you are working with—stones or wood chips are usually biggest. Add these to the center of the material.

Next, add any smaller dried herbs (including your flower), resins, or chips. Top these off with three drops of any essential oils you use. Drip them onto a dried herb or piece of wood so they soak into those instead of just the material.

Remember to focus on your vision of healing as you work. Imagine the energy of yourself being healed. What does it feel like? What emotions does being healed evoke for you? Pour those feelings and energies into your talisman.

When you are done filling it, bunch the material up into a pouch and wrap the brown ribbon around the neck three times before knotting it off. As you wrap and tie the ribbon, say:

What I command, make it be.
I bid these energies to work for me.
What I wish,
So toke it be.

Take a hit and release your intention and exhale your smoke all over the pouch. (You may also use the smoke from cannabis incense along with your own breath.)

Trim off any extra ribbon. Carry this talisman with you when you want to reharness or utilize these healing energies.

FEBRUARY 3
SOULFUL SEARCHING

Get high, meditate, and journal to explore what courage means to you. How do you personally define courage? What specific examples can you give? Has your vision of courage changed over the years, and if so, how? How important is the concept of courage to you? Where have you had the most courage in your life? In what ways have you found courage elusive?

FEBRUARY 4
ASTROLOGICAL HOUSES

Research the meaning of the astrological second house and explore the role it plays in your life within your own chart. The second house represents your money, finances, and possessions. Record the information you learn and how it relates to your sign and yourself in your Book of Shadows or a journal.

FEBRUARY 5
DELIGHTFUL DABBLING

Give yourself a boost of courage and confidence with this quick spell.

You will need:

- Small red candle (birthday, spell, or chime size)
- Lighter
- Cannabis incense (optional for nonsmokers)

Before you light the candle, smoke your weed (or use another consumption method) as you think about being confident and brave. Exhale the smoke onto the candle to charge the candle with your intentions. (You may also use smoke from cannabis incense.) Place the candle in a safe place and light it.

Stare into the flame of the candle. Think about the force of the heat, the power of fire. Imagine yourself harnessing that power and infusing it with confidence. As the flame burns, your infused intentions are released into the universe.

When the candle is almost done, light up your weed again and exhale your intentions as you blow out the flame. (You may also use the smoke from cannabis incense along with your own breath.)

FEBRUARY 6
CERRIDWEN'S CAULDRON

Explore a pantheon, the deities of a particular people (for example, Greek, Roman, Celtic, or Hindu), you are unfamiliar with and know little about. Stretch your comfort zone when you pick one to learn about. What about this pantheon interests you? Why do you believe you have not learned about this pantheon? Who in this pantheon do you find yourself connected to as you delve into this new world? Does this pantheon have a relationship with cannabis or other sacred smokables? Document the information you learn in your BOS.

FEBRUARY 7
LIFTED PERSPECTIVE

Connect with your higher self in a meditative state. Step back and look at yourself objectively; allow your walls to slip away.

Think about the type of healing you need to bring into your life. Is it physical, emotional, spiritual? Listen to what your higher self has to say to you. Let it tell you what you have been missing or avoiding. Let it tell you where healing needs to happen in your life. Listen to the advice from your higher self on where to begin this healing journey. Journal about your meditation.

FEBRUARY 8
MAGICAL MUSICAL MOVEMENT

Get yourself to a good, elevated, happy high (sativa or a hybrid recommended), accompanied by some fun, upbeat music to boost your mood and energy. Dance if you want to build even more energy. Focus on what courage looks like to you. Brainstorm what ultimate courage in your life would look like. Where do you show courage? Where do you wish to display more? See yourself as courageous and send it out into the universe. Build a playlist to use whenever you need to bring some courage into your life.

FEBRUARY 9
FIND YOUR WILD

Get into a good, comfortable, meditative high. Envision your idea of a courageous wild animal, living in its own environment. What animal do you choose? Where does this animal live? What about this animal do you find courageous? How can you emulate these ideas of courage in your own life? What lesson does this animal have for you?

After your meditation, research the spiritual significance of the animal you chose and journal about what you discover about your animal and yourself.

FEBRUARY 10
INTRIGUING INCANTATIONS

This healing chant can be used with any of your healing spellwork or on its own. Light up and focus on conjuring healing energies when you use it. Say:

> *By the earth, the fire, the water, and air,*
> *I call healing energies to appear.*
> *Mix and mingle, gather near.*
> *Heal me now; heal me here.*

If you are using this chant to infuse magic into an item, place your hand over it, focus, and visualize the energy flow through your hand into it on the "here" part of the chant. You can do this to infuse energy into things for immediate use or to "store" the energy for use later.

You can also visualize healing energies blending with the smoke from your weed to create a healing atmosphere around you.

FEBRUARY 11
EMBRACING THE ELEMENTS

Light your cannabis in whichever manner you prefer to smoke or vape it. (You may also observe the smoke from cannabis incense.) Focus on the air and the path it takes as you inhale. Follow this path in your mind. Smell the smoke or vapor. Feel the air as it fills your lungs. As you exhale, follow the path the air takes again. Feel the air leave your lungs and exit your body through your nose. This is the energy of air. Its presence is necessary for life. Meditate on the power of air in connection to your use of it with cannabis.

FEBRUARY 12
SUPERNATURAL SENSES

Subjective clairvoyance is when an image is seen in the mind's eye, also known as the *third eye*, and not with the physical eyes. It may appear fuzzy, come and go in a flash, or seem like a vivid dream. How these images appear is different for different people. You may also notice a difference in how entities present themselves. Certain ones may appear on the fuzzy side, while others are more tuned in and clear.

Seeing things, even if it's "all in your head," can be scary and confusing. These feelings lead to suppression of the skill. Weed may be beneficial to help regain or build the subjective clairvoyance skill.

What has been your experience with subjective clairvoyance so far? Document any experiences you have had (or have in the future) in your Book of Shadows.

Get as high as you like and try this exercise to see what comes to your mind. Either sit closely to a blank white wall or hold a piece of white paper closely in front of your eyes. Focus on the white blankness in front of your eyes for three minutes. Take deep breaths through your nose and concentrate on opening your third eye. When the three minutes are up, close your eyes. What appears in your mind's eye?

If you are interested in this, be sure to add this topic to your research list to gather more information.

FEBRUARY 13
RECLAIMING THE SHADOW

This month we have been focusing on several types of healing and courageous energies. Shadow work very much encompasses the courage to heal. Shadow work *is* the courage to heal; it is when we go deeply into ourselves to discover what it is we need to heal. We perform shadow work because we have the courage to heal the deep cuts and wounds.

Achieve a deep meditative state and open your mind to allow your higher self to show you the next steps in your healing journey. Your higher self will show you where you need to focus your courage and healing energies. After your meditation, journal about what you were shown and where your path is leading you.

FEBRUARY 14
DELIGHTFUL DABBLING

Partake in this day to celebrate love by honoring the love you have for yourself.

You will need:

- Mirror
- Pink candle

- Rosebuds (dried)

- Lighter

Sit in a comfortable position where you will be able to look in the mirror. Place the pink candle in front of you.

Smoke your weed in a fifty-fifty combination with the rose petals. (Alternately, make a hot rose herbal infusion and add your cannabis or THC concentrate to it.)

Light the candle. Take several deep breaths and look into your own eyes in the mirror. Have a conversation with yourself. Tell yourself all the things you love about you.

If you have problems getting started, try the ABC method—naming a reason for each letter of the alphabet.

When you are done, give yourself a hug and treat yourself to something special.

FEBRUARY 15
SOULFUL SEARCHING

While we often associate vulnerabilities with weakness, there is much for us to learn from them to help us grow. Slip into a comfortably high meditative state and the point of view of your higher self. Allow your walls to fall away, and find yourself in a safe, sacred space. Here you can face your vulnerabilities objectively. Dealing with vulnerabilities requires courage. Healing these vulnerabilities requires courage.

What vulnerability does your higher self want you to take on and face? Embrace your Achilles' heel. Meditate and journal on this aspect of your healing journey.

FEBRUARY 16
SACRED SMOKE

Holy basil is known for its healing, calming, and restorative energies. Combining it with an indica or indica-dominant hybrid may help increase its calming powers, while combining it with a sativa or sativa-dominant hybrid may increase its restorative energies, leaving you feeling more vibrantly refreshed.

Introduce yourself to holy basil by using it on its own several times, first exploring it with all your senses. How does it look? Smell? Feel? Taste? You may either smoke it or make a tealike infusion to drink by soaking the leaves in hot water.

How does it affect you? What do you feel when using it? How long does it take to feel the effects? How long do the effects last?

Evaluate and learn how holy basil works with your body and mind. Document this information in your Book of Shadows.

Once you become familiar with this herb, combine it with cannabis and again explore the effects, being sure to document your results. This herb can be combined with others to create blends.

FEBRUARY 17
KITCHEN WITCHERY

Boost your healing and make your home smell great with this antibacterial simmer pot. In the morning, combine the following ingredients in a pot of water to simmer throughout the day.

You will need:

- 1 apple sliced into thin rounds
- 1 orange sliced into thin rounds
- 9 cloves
- 3 cinnamon sticks
- ¼ cup pine needles
- 1 tablespoon whole allspice
- 1 tablespoon ground ginger
- ½ tablespoon coriander
- ½ tablespoon dried thyme
- 1 teaspoon white ground pepper
- Pinch of cannabis

As you prepare the ingredients and add them to the pot, pour intention into your work. Focus on whatever type of healing you need, whether it be physical, emotional, or spiritual—these healing energies blend for overall better health.

Keep the pot on a low flame on a back burner. Stir the pot nine times clockwise once every hour throughout the day.

Each time you stir the pot, say:

Fire, water, earth, and air,
My magic has a little flare.
Fruits from the earth simmer here.
Send your energies everywhere.

Add more water as needed to replenish what has evaporated. At the end of the day, pour the remains outside on the ground near a tree or under a bush. Return the plant material to the earth it came from. Add this recipe to your BOS and record your own experience with it.

FEBRUARY 18
DANK DIVINATION

This spread helps you to combine courage and healing to assist you on your own journey of growth.

Smoke a bowl, open your mind, and as you shuffle your tarot or oracle deck, blow smoke across your cards. (If you do not smoke or vape, you may use the smoke of cannabis-scented incense and get high with another consumption method.) Connect with your higher self or power and lay out five cards for the following interpretations:

Card 1. This card represents where you are in your spiritual journey.

Card 2. This card represents forces for or against your path to courageousness.

Card 3. This card represents forces for or against your path to healing.

Card 4. This card represents the next step in your journey.

Card 5. This card represents the next lesson to focus on.

Document your drawn cards and their meanings in your journal. Explore your reading in meditation.

FEBRUARY 19
ETHEREAL ESSENCES

Research the different correspondences and uses associated with sandalwood and add a supply to your witch's cupboard. Add the information you find to your BOS.

Meet the essence of sandalwood in the following meditative practice.

Get into an elevated high and comfortable position with a small container of dried sandalwood, a bottle of sandalwood oil, or sandalwood incense lit and placed in front of you.

Close your eyes and take several deep breaths. Allow your mind to settle and focus. When you are ready, pick up the sandalwood and hold it about four inches away from your nose. Inhale the scent, breathing deeply. If it's not too overpowering for you, move it closer. Some people have sensitivities, so don't feel you have to move it directly under your nose. Oils are very potent and do not need to be as close.

How does this scent make you feel? Is it pleasing? Irritating? Relaxing? Exciting? Powerful? Meditate on the feelings it evokes in you.

Journal about your experience. If you feel the need to clear the scent from your nose, sniff coffee beans or grounds to help neutralize the scent.

FEBRUARY 20
HERBAL INFUSIONS

Combine the following together to make an herbal restorative tea to help boost your immune system and warm your spirit.

- 1 cup thoroughly cooked elderberries (to remove toxicity)
- 1 teaspoon crushed (not ground) allspice
- 1 teaspoon ground cinnamon
- 2 teaspoons whole cloves

Place the ingredients together in a container and blend well. Use a teaspoon at a time in a tea ball, steeped for three to five minutes in hot water.

FEBRUARY 21
GROWING WITH THE GREEN MAN

The Green Man can be hidden in plain sight as he hides and camouflages himself with nature.

Get high and meet with your higher self or power in meditation. What opportunities in your life are present but camouflaged or hidden? Take a step back and look to see what you are missing. Let your higher self or power show you the forest instead of only the trees.

FEBRUARY 22
DELIGHTFUL DABBLING

Grind your buds for individual spellwork each time they are needed so you can personalize them with focused intention. As you grind your buds, set your intentions into them. If you like, have a specific grinder for your magical workings.

Use chants while grinding, filling bowls, rolling joints, or other preparation methods to help set intentions. How can you implement these practices into your daily life?

FEBRUARY 23
RECLAIMING THE SHADOW

Slip into a meditative state. Lower your walls and either step into your higher self or connect with your higher power.

Cotton mouth is a common occurrence for some smokers. It's unpleasant, dry, bland, and can be bothersome. It's also a temporary condition. What unpleasantness do you have in your own life? What is dry, bland, or otherwise uninteresting? What needs freshening up?

After your meditation, journal about your experience and brainstorm steps to take to rid yourself of your own cotton mouth.

FEBRUARY 24
DANK DIVINATION

Reading tea leaves, *tasseography*, is an ancient practice you can add to your own personal divination practice. While certain symbols may have specific meanings, your own connotation is extremely—if not more—important for your personal work. You do not need to have a ton of practice in reading tea leaves to read your own. Keep an open and objective mind while working from your higher self for this exercise.

You will need:

- 1 teaspoon dried mugwort
- 1 teaspoon dried cannabis flower

Mix up a cup of mugwort and cannabis flower tea, leaving the leaves loose in your cup. For best results, do not use boiling water; keep it below 160 degrees, and use decarboxylated flower if you can to ensure you will get a high from this infusion. You can add THC oil if you wish to boost your high, but you want enough plant material that can steep and then form an image at the bottom of your cup.

Relax and allow your mind to open as you gently sip your tea. Focus on the question, What message does the universe have for you? When you are down to the last sip of your tea, swirl the liquid and the plant material three times clockwise. Use your higher power or self to help you decipher what you see.

Record your experience in your Book of Shadows and add any information you learn about tasseography.

FEBRUARY 25
MEDITATION MOJO

Find a comfortable high for your meditation.

The budtender represents a caring individual, one who helps you to be the best version of yourself. They let you know when your bong water stinks; aka, they call you out on your own crap but also know when to sit back and chill. Who is the budtender in your life? How do they fit the role?

FEBRUARY 26
HERBAL BLENDS

Boost your self-healing with this herbal blend. Smoke it with your cannabis or make it into a tea.

You will need:

- Lavender buds (dried)
- Sacred lotus petals (dried)
- Rose petals (dried)

Blend together dried lavender buds, sacred lotus petals, and rose petals in equal ratios, and grind together in a grinder. Combine this with your ground flower in a one-to-one ratio. As you combine and grind your herbs together, focus on the healing you are seeking.

Use this blend when you need to show yourself compassion, love, and support. Add this recipe to your Book of Shadows and record your experiences with it. If you desire, adjust ratios for flavor.

FEBRUARY 27
FIND YOUR WILD

Connect to the night sky with a good high. You do not have to see the stars with your physical eyes if you picture them in your mind's eye. A galaxy map can show you where you are in relation to constellations and the moon to help you get your bearings and give you images to visualize.

Stand outside in the dark with your face to the sky. Either stare into space, taking in everything you can see—the stars, the moon, even satellites and airplanes cutting across the sky—or if it is too cloudy or your view is disrupted by light pollution, picture them in your mind. The energies of air and celestial bodies are all around you. How do these energies feel to you? How do you differentiate them from one another? How can you best utilize them? Add this information to your BOS.

This exercise will be done monthly throughout the year because as the night sky changes, the energies you feel will also change.

FEBRUARY 28
SOULFUL SEARCHING

Settle into a comfortable high and look back over the past month. What types of healing did you work with? Where did you feel the most successful in your healing journey? Where do you find you still need work? Meditate on and journal about your growth and progress.

FEBRUARY 29
DELIGHTFUL DABBLING

Leap year is a liminal time that only happens once every four years. It is a wonderful day to use your imagination to slip into a different realm of fantasy, or alternate reality—however you prefer to see it.

Enhance your trip by adding dried mugwort to your cannabis in a fifty-fifty blend to smoke. (Alternately, you may make mugwort tea and add your cannabis or THC to it, or consume it in your regular manner.)

Lie down in a comfortable position, add music if you like, say, "Take me away," and let your high slip you into a liminal space.

After your sesh, journal about where you went, what or whom you saw, and what you did there.

March

Spring is on its way, and the time of rebirth and renewal is at hand. This month, you will take on new challenges and find how it helps to have luck on your side, along with a boost of courage to help you through struggles.

March Supply List
March 2

Green air-dry clay (either purchase or make your own)

Dragon's blood essential oil

Carrier oil (optional)

Cannabis (dried)

Allspice (ground)

Cinnamon (ground)

Clove (ground)

Clay carving utensil

Olive leaf outline

Silver paint and paintbrush or silver paint marker (optional)

March 8

Glass jar with lid or corked vial

Dried: cannabis, magnolia, carnation, white chrysanthemum, daisy petals, sage, motherwort, blue
lotus petals, sacred lotus petals, sandalwood

Cloves

Moss agate chips

Red sealing wax

Black sealing wax

March 14

Cannabis incense (optional for nonsmokers)

March 15

Clear quartz

Cannabis incense (optional for nonsmokers)

March 16

Calea zacatechichi

March 18

Glass jar with lid or corked vial

Cannabis ash

Orange calcite chips

Bloodstone chips

Carnelian chips

Dried: catnip, garlic, lavender, rosemary, crushed red
pepper, thistle

Clove

Frankincense

Black peppercorn

Paper (optional)

Writing instrument (optional)

Red sealing wax

Orange sealing wax

March 19

Bergamot

March 20

Dried: chamomile, peppermint, St. John's wort,
spearmint

March 24

Black or dark colored bowl

Moon water

2 black candles

Lighter

Obsidian stone

Cannabis incense (optional for nonsmokers)

March 25

Cedar chips or shavings

Thorns from a hawthorn tree

Dried or fresh: holly leaves, chamomile

Clover

Dried or fresh petals or essential oil: bluebells, daffodils, daisies, heather, jasmine, lavender, lilac, lotus, rose, violet

Cannabis

March 26

Ground: allspice, cinnamon

Vanilla bean (dried, crushed)

MARCH 1
LIT LITERATURE

Your assignment this month is to explore as many different goddesses as you can through brief introductions to them. Do not focus on books dedicated to an individual goddess; instead, look for titles that cover at least a couple dozen. Take note of any specific goddesses who catch your attention for further research later.

No matter where you shop for books, use the keywords "goddesses" or "books on goddesses" in your search to find titles of interest. Add any additional titles that pique your interest to your to-be-read list.

MARCH 2
TEMPTING TALISMAN

Create this luck-of-the-draw talisman to carry with you when you need Lady Luck on your side.

You will need:

- Green air-dry clay (either purchase or make your own)
- Dragon's blood essential oil (Mix with a carrier oil first or wear plastic gloves if you wish.)
- Carrier oil (optional)

- Cannabis
- Allspice (ground)
- Cinnamon (ground)
- Clove (ground)
- Clay carving utensil
- Olive leaf outline (optional)
- Silver paint and paintbrush or silver paint marker (optional)

Begin by warming your clay by working with it a bit in your hands, playing with it between your fingers and palms, while focusing on infusing your energy into the clay. When you are ready, slightly flatten it out and add a drop of dragon's blood oil to the center. Top off with a small pinch each of the ground cannabis flower, allspice, cinnamon, and clove. Fold the clay up and begin working it again, blending the energies into the clay.

Form the clay into a shape that suits you and your skill level. A flattened circle or oval shape works, or you may be more elaborate and form a four-leaf clover or cannabis leaf. Using the carving tool, draw the olive leaf into the clay to symbolize drawing luck to you. Use an outline of the shape as a stencil if you'd like.

When you are finished with your talisman, vape or smoke your cannabis to pass it through the smoke (or use cannabis incense). This gives your talisman an extra boost of your personal energy combined with the energies of the weed.

Allow at least twenty-four hours for your clay to dry. If you like, you may paint or outline the olive leaf with silver paint or a paint marker and let it dry again.

Carry your talisman with you when a bit of extra luck is desired.

MARCH 3
SOULFUL SEARCHING

Get high, meditate, and journal on what the concept of nurturing the self means to you. How do you personally define nurturing the self? What specific examples can you give? Has your definition changed over the years, and if so, how? How important is it to you to nurture yourself? In what ways have you found nurturing yourself difficult?

MARCH 4
ASTROLOGICAL HOUSES

Research the meaning of the astrological third house and explore the role it plays in your life within your own chart. The third house represents communication. Record the information you learn and how it relates to your sign and yourself in your Book of Shadows or a journal.

MARCH 5
EMBRACING THE ELEMENTS

Graveyard dirt is used in hexes, curses, protection, divination, and even love spells. When collecting graveyard dirt, leave an offering in exchange and work with your own ancestors when it is possible.

Though you can find graveyard dirt for sale, you don't know its authenticity or history. Brainstorm and list places where you could safely and respectfully obtain graveyard dust in your Book of Shadows.

MARCH 6
CERRIDWEN'S CAULDRON

Spend this month either collecting or refreshing your information on foundational correspondences. Research the days of the week, where their names came from, and what the qualities are for each one.

Next, brush up on your color correspondences knowledge and document this information in your BOS. Depending on the strain, cannabis flowers may be either green or purple.

Include some of your favorite green and purple strain names to boost your magical energy with your color information.

Having pipes, bongs, rolling papers, and other equipment available in a variety of colors is an additional way to add color magic to your workings.

MARCH 7
LIFTED PERSPECTIVE

Get high and into a meditative state to connect with your higher self. Let down the walls and see yourself and your actions from an objective point of view. Think back to a situation you are not proud of. Even though you may not be proud of something, it may have much to teach you. Look at this situation from your higher perspective. What lesson is there for you to learn from the situation? How can you approach or respond to similar situations differently in the future? Forgive yourself if necessary. Journal about your experience.

MARCH 8
DELIGHTFUL DABBLING

The truth is on your side, but sometimes you need to find it first. What truth are you searching for? Create this spell jar to help shine a light on the truth you seek.

You will need:

- Glass jar with lid or corked vial
- Cannabis (dried)
- Magnolia (dried)
- Carnation (dried)
- White chrysanthemum (dried)
- Daisy petals (dried)
- Sage (dried)
- Motherwort (dried)
- Blue lotus petals (dried)
- Sacred lotus petals (dried)
- Sandalwood (dried)
- Cloves
- Moss agate chips
- Red sealing wax
- Black sealing wax

Smoke your weed (or use another consumption method, allowing time for edibles to take effect).

Place each ingredient into your chosen jar (or mix them in a bowl and then transfer them to your jar), focusing on each one's energy along with your intention. Focus on the truth you seek as you build and bless your jar.

As you work with each ingredient, say:

I call upon the energies of [ingredient name],
Bring the truth to me.

What truth are you seeking? Write your questions on a piece of paper and place it in the jar.

Take a hit (or deep, centered, intention-filled breath if you do not smoke or vape) and use your exhalation to gently blow your hopes and objectives into your jar.

Close the top of the jar and cover it with melted sealing wax, first the black and then the red. When finished, say:

In this vessel,
Combine together,
Bring the truth to me.
In this vessel,
Combine together,
The truth is what I see.

Place your jar next to your bed while you sleep or in a place where you will frequently see it or be close to it.

MARCH 9
FIND YOUR WILD

Spring is almost officially here. How can you see and feel the changes of the seasons where you live? Does your weather change? Do plants go dormant? Do animals migrate to or away from you? What amount of daylight do you experience? What shifts in energy can you discover?

Depending on where you live, the changes you see between seasons may be very subtle or a bit drastic. Step outside and pay attention today to what you experience and feel in the environment around you as you begin the final shift from winter into spring. Try detecting energies around you both before and after you get high. What differences do you notice?

MARCH 10
EMBRACING THE ELEMENTS

It is the female plant that gives us big, beautiful flowers to smoke, but male plants also have their own uses. While cloning female plants is popular, male plants are necessary to produce and harvest seeds that can be used for growing new plants or as a food source. Learn and identify the parts of male and female cannabis plants.

MARCH 11
GROWING WITH THE GREEN MAN

Get high and take a stroll through your own neighborhood. What signs of life can you find other than humans? What kinds of plant life do you find? What kinds of animal life? Even bugs count! Take in the different life-forms you encounter. What types of energies do you detect from these other living beings?

MARCH 12
SUPERNATURAL SENSES

Clairaudience is the hearing of sounds not detected by the human ear. These sounds may be heard like a whisper coming from right over your shoulder or a voice inside your head, often near the inner ear area. While sometimes they are quiet, other times it sounds like someone just yelled your name only for you to turn and find no one there.

Cannabis helps to lower the walls and make the connection so that clairaudience can be easier to access, particularly when in a deeply meditative state. Open your higher self to listening to messages from Spirit or the spirit world.

Consume your weed and sit either outside or near an open window. Listen to everything around you. Single out each sound you hear, acknowledge it, and let it move on from your attention. Eliminate each sound until the only sound left is the breeze of the air around you. Focus on this sound only and listen for messages in the wind.

Document your past experiences in your BOS and be sure to update it as new occurrences happen. If you are interested in this, be sure to add clairaudience to your research list to gather more information.

MARCH 13
RECLAIMING THE SHADOW

Achieve a deep meditative high. Connect with your higher self or power.

Bong water is stinky, residue-filled, nasty stuff. If it doesn't get cleaned frequently, it builds up into a horrible, difficult-to-clean-up mess. When you don't pay attention to yourself, you may also build up some stinky residue. Get this stink out of your life. What is cloudy in your life due to a lack of maintenance in your past? Clear out the old, cleanse, refresh, and make way for the new. Journal about your experience and brainstorm your next steps.

MARCH 14
DANK DIVINATION

This spread uses the form of a full-grown, healthy cola to assist you on your own journey of growth.

Smoke a bowl, open your mind, and as you shuffle your tarot or oracle deck, blow smoke across your cards. (If you do not smoke or vape, you may use the smoke of cannabis-scented incense and get high with another consumption method.) Connect with your higher self or power and lay out seven cards as shown.

Card 1. You and your current situation.

Card 2. Basis of your growth.

Card 3. How the past affects the basis of your growth.

Card 4. How unseen and unknown events affect the basis of your growth.

Card 5. The pathway to take.

Card 6. Obstacles to watch for.

Card 7. Outlook of what is to come.

Document your drawn cards and their meanings in your journal. Explore your reading in meditation.

MARCH 15
DELIGHTFUL DABBLING

Cleanse your clear quartz with your weed smoke and intention.
You will need:

- Clear quartz
- Cannabis incense (optional for nonsmokers)

Hold your quartz in your hand and say:

I pour intention into my toke,
To cleanse this crystal with my smoke.

Shiny bright and crystal clear,
Dullness and negativity disappear.

As you inhale the smoke, focus on clear, cleansing energies as you exhale, blowing the smoke over the quartz and directing its energy to purge and dispel any negativity. (You may also use the smoke from cannabis incense.)

MARCH 16
SACRED SMOKE

Also known as the Mexican "dream herb," *Calea zacatechichi* (KUH-lee-UH za-KUH-teh-CHEE-CHEE) may induce lucid dreams along with dream recall, and it assists in connection with your higher self and the spirit world. When combined with an indica cannabis, the effects may increase exponentially.

Introduce yourself to *Calea zacatechichi* by using it on its own several times first, exploring it with all your senses. How does it look? Smell? Feel? Taste? You may either smoke it or make a tealike infusion by soaking the leaves in hot water to drink.

How does it affect you? What do you feel when using it? How long does it take to feel the effects? How long do the effects last?

Evaluate and learn how *Calea zacatechichi* works with your body and mind. Document this information in your Book of Shadows.

Once you become familiar with this herb, combine it with cannabis and again explore the effects, being sure to document your results. This herb can be combined with others to create blends, but it should not be used with certain medications. Be sure it is safe for your consumption.

MARCH 17
MAGICAL MUSICAL MOVEMENT

On this day to honor both the heritage and the luck of the Irish, celebrate it with a happy high and a playlist of Irish music. Whether Celtic harps or Irish pipes, jigs, or reels, appreciate a variety of musical styles. Dance and sing along if you wish, or simply relax in your high. Either way, soak in the music of Irish culture and enjoy.

MARCH 18
DELIGHTFUL DABBLING

Create this spell jar to carry with you the next time you need an extra dose of courage.

You will need:

- Glass jar with lid or corked vial
- Cannabis ash
- Orange calcite chips
- Bloodstone chips
- Carnelian chips
- Catnip (dried)
- Garlic (dried)
- Lavender (dried)
- Rosemary (dried)
- Crushed red pepper (dried)
- Thistle (dried)
- Clove
- Frankincense
- Black peppercorn
- Paper (optional)
- Writing instrument (optional)
- Red sealing wax
- Orange sealing wax

Smoke your weed (or use another consumption method, allowing time for edibles to take effect).

Place each ingredient into your chosen jar (or mix them in a bowl and then transfer them to your jar), focusing on each one's energy along with your intention. Visualize your courageous self as you build and bless your jar.

As you work with each ingredient, say:

I call upon the energies of [ingredient name],
Come to me and stand at my side.

If you have a specific event or incident you wish to boost your courage for, write it on a piece of paper and place it in the jar.

Take a hit (or deep, centered, intention-filled breath if you do not smoke or vape) and use your exhalation to gently blow your objectives into your jar.

Close the top of the jar and cover it with melted sealing wax, first the red and then the orange. When finished, say:

In this vessel,
Energies together,
My courage makes me bold.
When this power is needed,
It is in my grasp to hold.

Carry your jar or vial with you when you need the extra dose of courage backing you up.

MARCH 19
ETHEREAL ESSENCES

Research the different correspondences and uses associated with bergamot and add a supply to your witch's cupboard. Add the information you find to your BOS. Dried bergamot can be smoked, combined with cannabis, or made into a tea. Meet the essence of bergamot in the following meditative practice.

Get into an elevated high and comfortable position with a small container of dried bergamot, a bottle of bergamot oil, or bergamot incense lit and placed in front of you.

Close your eyes and take several deep breaths. Allow your mind to settle and focus. When you are ready, pick up the bergamot and hold it about four inches away from your nose. Inhale the scent, breathing deeply. If it's not too overpowering for you, move it closer. Some people have sensitivities, so don't feel you have to move it directly under your nose. Oils are very potent and do not need to be moved as close.

How does this scent make you feel? Is it pleasing? Irritating? Relaxing? Exciting? Powerful? Meditate on the feelings it evokes in you.

Journal about your experience. If you feel the need to clear the scent from your nose, sniff coffee beans or grounds to help neutralize the scent.

MARCH 20
HERBAL INFUSIONS

Combine the following together to make an herbal tea to draw luck into your life. As you sip your infusion, focus on the specific situation where luck is needed.

- 1 cup chamomile (dried)
- ½ cup peppermint (dried)
- ¼ cup St. John's wort (dried)
- ¼ cup spearmint (dried)

You can either steep the blend with dried ground cannabis or add a concentrate (such as an oil or tincture) at your desired dosage.

Place the ingredients together in a container and blend well. Use two teaspoons at a time in a tea ball, steeped for three to five minutes in hot water.

MARCH 21
VIBING

Energy is information that moves. Cannabis is a type of earth energy that helps you tune in to different frequencies by changing your vibration. When your vibration changes, you have access to additional information.

Experiment with various levels of being high. Pay focused attention to the changes in your own vibration as you climb into your higher self.

Meditate on this information and the changes you felt in yourself. Journal about your experience.

MARCH 22
SOULFUL SEARCHING

Healthy boundaries are important for healthy relationships—not only with others, but for the relationship you have with yourself. Where do you find chaos in your life? Where are there issues keeping things under control? What boundaries can you set in place in your life to smooth out issues that are not in your control? Spend time meditating and journaling to produce three new boundary statements to live by.

MARCH 23
RECLAIMING THE SHADOW

Reach a meditative state with your higher self and recall a time when you were wrong but didn't want to accept it. What held you back? What feelings did you experience? What have you learned since then? How could you handle a comparable situation now? Journal about your experience.

MARCH 24
DANK DIVINATION

Use this divination session to interpret messages through water.

You will need:

- Black or dark colored bowl
- Moon water
- 2 black candles
- Lighter
- Obsidian stone
- Cannabis incense (optional for nonsmokers)

In a dark or dimly lit room, use a dark (preferably black) bowl and fill it with moon water. Light two black candles and place them to the back left and right of the bowl, about six inches away. Place an obsidian stone in the center of the bowl.

Smoke or vape your weed, and as you exhale, gently blow the smoke across the surface of the water (or blow the smoke from cannabis incense) and open your mind to receiving images through the reflections of the water.

Record your experience in your Book of Shadows along with any information you obtain through research on water scrying.

MARCH 25
KITCHEN WITCHERY

In the morning, combine the following ingredients in a pot of water to simmer throughout the day. This simmer pot is filled with flowers to draw good luck to you and perfume your home. Use no more than a small handful (do not crush or squeeze) of each petal type or a couple drops of each oil.

You will need:

- ¼ cup cedar chips or shavings
- 3 thorns from a hawthorn tree
- 3 holly leaves (dried or fresh)
- 1 tablespoon chamomile (dried or fresh)
- 1 tablespoon clover (fresh is best if it grows nearby)
- Bluebells (dried or fresh petals or essential oil)
- Daffodils (dried or fresh petals or essential oil)
- Daisies (dried or fresh petals or essential oil)
- Heather (dried or fresh petals or essential oil)
- Jasmine (dried or fresh petals or essential oil)

- Lavender (dried or fresh petals or essential oil)
- Lilac (dried or fresh petals or essential oil)
- Lotus (dried or fresh petals or essential oil)
- Rose (dried or fresh petals or essential oil)
- Violet (dried or fresh petals or essential oil)
- Pinch of cannabis

As you prepare the ingredients and add them to the pot, pour intention into your work. Focus on drawing good luck into your life.

Keep the pot on a low flame on a back burner. Stir the pot nine times clockwise once every hour throughout the day.

Each time you stir the pot, say:

Fire, water, earth, and air,
My magic has a little flare.
Fruits from the earth simmer here.
Good luck I command to appear.

Add more water as needed to replenish what has evaporated. At the end of the day, pour the remains outside on the ground near a tree or under a bush. Return the plant material to the earth it came from. Add this recipe to your BOS and record your own experience with it.

MARCH 26
HERBAL BLENDS

Spice up your luck with this blend.

You will need:

- Allspice (ground)
- Cinnamon (ground)
- Vanilla bean (dried, crushed)

Sprinkle ground allspice, ground cinnamon, and a bit of dried, crushed vanilla bean on top of your weed. To mix into a blend, add ¼ teaspoon of each ingredient to an eighth of dried, ground bud. This blend can be smoked or brewed into tea.

Use this blend on its own for a boost or to accompany your success-themed spellwork. Focus on the success you are seeking as you combine and grind your herbs together, infusing the blend with your intention and energy.

Add this recipe, how it feels, and your results to your Book of Shadows. If you desire, adjust ratios for flavor.

MARCH 27
FIND YOUR WILD

Connect to the night sky with a good high. You do not have to see the stars with your physical eyes if you picture them in your mind's eye. A galaxy map can show you where you are in relation to constellations and the moon to help you get your bearings and give you images to visualize.

Stand outside in the dark with your face to the sky. Either stare into space, taking in everything you can see—the stars, the moon, even satellites and airplanes cutting across the sky—or if it is too cloudy or your view is disrupted by light pollution, picture them in your mind. The energies of air and celestial bodies are all around you. How do these energies feel to you? How do you differentiate them from one another? How can you best utilize them? Add this information to your BOS.

This exercise will be done monthly throughout the year because as the night sky changes, the energies you feel will also change.

MARCH 28
MAGICAL MUSICAL MOVEMENT

Start a playlist of songs with the themes of renewal, rejuvenation, and rebirth. Think spring. What songs give you a bouncy, renewed energy for life? This playlist can be used during prep and spellwork or other workings. Be sure to check out frequency-based music.

Try out your playlist by getting high and choosing a few songs to move to in whatever type of movement you prefer, even if it is only rocking back and forth.

Try listening to your playlist motionless with your eyes closed or with a blindfold to block out other distractions. Use headphones if possible. Does it create the energy and environment you desire?

MARCH 29
INTRIGUING INCANTATIONS

At certain times in life, you will find it beneficial to have luck on your side. Use this chant to draw it in when a little extra is called for. Light your weed, focus on what type of luck is needed, and say:

By the earth, the fire, the water, and air,
I pull in energies from here and there.
The luck I need, send it here,
Bring it close, bring it near,
Within my grasp for me to be blessed.
The luck I need is my quest.

Repeat it as often as you want.

MARCH 30
DELIGHTFUL DABBLING

Increase your magic and the focus of your intention by writing sigils, runes, words, or symbols on rolling papers with nontoxic ink, such as with edible markers or pens.

Form your weed into a symbol on a rolling tray or charging plate before use to infuse it with more energy. Use narrow crystal points that match your intention as tools to maneuver the ground bud into place. How can you implement these practices into your daily life?

MARCH 31
SOULFUL SEARCHING

This month you worked with both luck and courage, a winning combination to open new opportunities for yourself. How can you use these concepts to form your future? Meditate and journal on your overall experiences and how they contributed to your practice, spirituality, or both.

April

April is the first full month of spring, and in climates where much of nature goes dormant (or migrates) for the winter, the signs of rebirth abound. The light from the sun grows, darkness is dispelled, and life begins anew. Spring is the time for love and hope. As the energies of the natural world shift, so do we.

April Supply List
April 2

> 5 × 5-inch square piece of pink material
>
> Bloodstone, small piece or a few chips
>
> Rose quartz, small piece or a few chips
>
> Essential oil, dried herb, or resin: carnation, honeysuckle, rose, violet, frankincense, myrrh, cannabis
>
> 6 inches of silver string or ribbon

April 8

Glass jar with lid or corked vial

Dried: rose petals, lavender buds, blue lotus petals,
   motherwort, damiana, holy basil, cannabis

Himalayan pink salt

Sugar

Small chunk of dark chocolate

Cinnamon

Aquamarine chips

Rose quartz chips

Pink sealing wax

April 12

Ginger

April 14

Cannabis incense (optional for nonsmokers)

April 16

Mullein

April 17

Dried or fresh: chamomile buds, clover buds, jasmine flowers, lavender buds, strawberries, raspberries, cannabis

April 18

Rose quartz

April 19

Lime

April 22

Glass jar with lid or corked vial

Dragon's blood (resin or powdered incense)

Gold flakes (for cake decorating)

Silver flakes (for cake decorating)

Dried: chamomile, clover, hibiscus, jasmine, lavender, rose petals, cannabis

Lapis lazuli chips

Moonstone chips

Quartz chips

Rose quartz chips

Pink sealing wax

Enough red twine to wrap around the top of your
jar and tie on a charm

Heart-shaped charm

April 24

2 black candles

Lighter

Obsidian stone

Cannabis incense (optional for nonsmokers)

April 26

Dried: motherwort, damiana, sacred lotus petals,
rose petals, bergamot

APRIL 1
LIT LITERATURE

Cannabis and hemp have been used for hundreds of years
for a variety of purposes, from medicine to an entheogen,
to linens, ropes, and sails. Today, the plant enjoys dozens of
uses. Expand your knowledge this month by learning about
different uses of cannabis and hemp.

No matter where you shop for books, use the keywords
"cannabis and hemp use" in your search to find titles of

interest. Add any additional titles that pique your interest to your to-be-read list.

APRIL 2
TEMPTING TALISMAN

As you create your talisman, focus on what love looks like for *you*. What type of love do you want to bring into your life? Self-love? The love of family? From a romantic partner? Focus on the love you want to attract as if it is already here. You *are* loved. The love you want is present in your life. Pour this energy into your talisman as you give it life.

Try to use a mix of oils and dried ingredients if available to you. Use a pinch of dried ingredients and a drop or two of oils.

You will need:

- 5 × 5-inch square piece of pink material
- Bloodstone, small piece or a few chips
- Rose quartz, small piece or a few chips
- Carnation (essential oil, dried herb, or resin)
- Honeysuckle (essential oil, dried herb, or resin)
- Rose (essential oil, dried herb, or resin)
- Violet (essential oil, dried herb, or resin)

- Frankincense (essential oil, dried herb, or resin)
- Myrrh (essential oil, dried herb, or resin)
- Cannabis (essential oil, dried herb, or resin)
- 6 inches of silver string or ribbon

Smoke your weed (or use another consumption method, allowing time for edibles to take effect) while you assemble your ingredients and create this talisman. If you have room to work at your altar, do so, or create another sacred space where you have room and are comfortable.

Lay the pink square on your altar or other stable location. Begin with the largest ingredients you are working with—stones or chips are usually biggest. Add these to the center of the material.

Next, add any smaller dried herbs (including your flower), resins, or chips. Top these off with one to two drops of any essential oils you use. Drip them onto a dried herb or resin so they soak into those instead of just the material.

Remember to focus on your vision of love as you work. What does it feel like? Pour these feelings and energies into your talisman.

When you are done filling it, bunch the material up into a pouch and wrap the silver string or ribbon around the neck three times before knotting it off. As you wrap and tie the ribbon, say:

The love I need,
Bring it to me.
This is my will.
So mote it be.

Trim off any extra ribbon. Carry this talisman with you or place it in a prominent location in your home to do its work and draw love into your life.

APRIL 3
SOULFUL SEARCHING

Get high, meditate, and then journal about how you cope (or don't) with rejection. What patterns do you follow? How can you break these patterns, and what new ones can you set for yourself? What good coping skills do you exhibit?

APRIL 4
ASTROLOGICAL HOUSES

Research the meaning of the astrological fourth house and explore the role it plays in your life within your own chart. The fourth house represents your family and home life. Record the information you learn and how it relates to your sign and yourself in your Book of Shadows or a journal.

APRIL 5
DELIGHTFUL DABBLING

What do you consider to be sacred ground? While this is often thought of as from a churchyard, you can create your own sacred ground by using the same area over and over for your workings. You create the sacred ground with your sacred workings.

Dirt from sacred ground is used in spells and workings for healing, justice, mending relationships, prosperity, protection, or purification, or as an offering. Brainstorm locations you can use for your sacred ground dirt and document them in your Book of Shadows.

APRIL 6
CERRIDWEN'S CAULDRON

Spring is associated with love, passion, and rebirth because these are all parts of the energies present in the natural world around us. Many animals and birds are welcoming offspring to their families. The days are growing longer, resulting in more daylight, which then means less melatonin and more serotonin in our bodies. We are biologically designed to become livelier and more energetic in the spring than we were in the winter.

This month, research both gods and goddesses of love, passion, and rebirth. Which ones resonate with you? Who would you like to work with, and what draws you to them? Do any of them have a known relationship with cannabis or other sacred smokables? Add all the information you discover along with your thoughts and impressions to your Book of Shadows.

APRIL 7
LIFTED PERSPECTIVE

Settle into a meditative high and position. Practicing looking at situations from different angles during meditation helps you develop this skill quickly to use in everyday life.

Imagine the ceiling of your dwelling is peeled back, exposing your home to the sky, while you are a giant looking down inside. Move from room to room, looking down from above. What do you observe?

APRIL 8
DELIGHTFUL DABBLING

Encourage and boost your own self love with this spell jar working.

You will need:

- Glass jar with lid or corked vial
- Rose petals (dried)
- Lavender buds (dried)
- Blue lotus petals (dried)
- Motherwort (dried)
- Damiana (dried)
- Holy basil (dried)
- Cannabis (dried)
- Himalayan pink salt
- Sugar
- Small chunk of dark chocolate
- Cinnamon
- Aquamarine chips
- Rose quartz chips
- Pink sealing wax

Smoke your weed (or use another consumption method, allowing time for edibles to take effect).

Place each ingredient into your chosen jar (or mix them in a bowl and then transfer them to your jar), focusing on each one's energy along with your intention. Visualize a loving bubble being created around you as you build and bless your jar.

As you work with each ingredient, say:

>*I call upon the energies of [ingredient name],*
>*Bring the power of positivity.*
>*Fill me with love,*
>*Especially when I need it most.*

Take a hit (or deep, centered, intention-filled breath if you do not smoke or vape) and use your exhalation to gently blow an expression of self-love and positivity into the jar.

Close the top of the jar and cover it with the melted pink sealing wax. When finished, say:

>*In this vessel,*
>*Combine together,*
>*Fill my heart with love.*
>*In this vessel,*
>*Combine together,*
>*Surround my heart with love.*

Carry your jar or vial with you or place it in a prominent location in your home, on your altar, or next to your bed. When you need a boost of self-love, hold it in your hand and envision a pink protective bubble around you, hugging you in love.

APRIL 9
FIND YOUR WILD

Find a place to take a nature break today and seek out the natural energies of spring. After you get high, spend at least fifteen minutes outside, preferably in a location with as few other people and distractions as possible. Close your eyes and tune out all human-caused energies around you. Eliminate manufactured sounds and scents. Allow yourself several minutes to adjust to the energies around you and shuffle through them, marking those you can for ignoring. What natural forces can you detect? What do you hear? What do you smell? What do you feel in the air?

APRIL 10
EMBRACING THE ELEMENTS

In this meditation, you will embrace each of the elements as you visualize yourself using a bong. If you like, use one to get high to help set your mood, or use another consumption method. Either way, you will visualize using a bong.

Each of the elements is represented when you smoke from a bong. Remember this as you prepare and smoke or consume another way.

Get into your meditative state and visualize yourself sitting with a big, round, crystal-clear glass bong in your lap in front of you. See the water splashing against the glass inside the bong. Imagine this water is crisp, clear, blessed full moon water containing the essence of your favorite herb or flower. This is the element of water. Your bowl is filled with beautiful, dried flower—your favorite strain in rich colors. The plant material is the element of earth. You light your hemp wick, bringing the element of fire to meet with earth. As you inhale, engaging the element of air, the water filters the smoke, which then combines all the elements together into you: spirit.

Feel the connection between each of the elements as you follow their path. Journal about your meditation experience.

APRIL 11
GROWING WITH THE GREEN MAN

While the dandelion exists almost everywhere on earth, chemical weed killer companies have demonized this beneficial, useful, and resilient plant. Dandelions are free food and medicine, and their roasted roots make a delicious hot herbal infusion.

From growing deep roots to freely blowing in the wind to spread seeds and wishes, the dandelion has much to teach us. If you can, sit outside with some dandelions in your high today. Otherwise, perform this meditation where you normally would. Slip into a high and visualize a dandelion in your mind. Connect with the spirit of the dandelion. What message does it have for you today?

APRIL 12
SUPERNATURAL SENSES

A sudden scent of flowers on a nonexistent breeze, rich roasted coffee beans though none are brewing, a powerful blast of cologne when you are all alone—clairalience is unexplainable scents and odors suddenly perceivable when there is no physical explanation for them. Perhaps a loved one's favorite scent hugs you in warmth in times of stress, or you've smelled something burning that *could* have caused a fire, but you got to it in time, the burning odor coming as a warning not a result.

Cannabis helps to lower the walls and make the connection so clairalience can be easier to access, particularly when in a deeply meditative state. Open your higher self to listening (or in this case, smelling!) for messages from Spirit or the spirit world.

Consume your weed. Take several deep breaths through your nose. Sniff some ginger to cleanse any other scents away, taking several deeper breaths to ensure a fresh start. As you breathe, open your mind to sensing through your sense of smell. Turn your head back and forth as you take in everything around you. What scents either come to mind or can you physically smell?

Document your experiences in your BOS and be sure to update it as new events occur. If you are interested in this, be sure to add this topic to your research list to gather more information.

APRIL 13
RECLAIMING THE SHADOW

Slip into a deep meditative high and connect with your higher power or self.

Choose a demanding situation in your life. Take the time to objectively examine the issue and possible points of view of other participants. See things for how they really are, not how you want them to be. How does your current view compare to the reality of the situation? Is the reality changeable? Accept the things you cannot change.

Journal about your experience. Include statements of acceptance for things you cannot change.

APRIL 14
DANK DIVINATION

This spread is all about being presented with a variety of options for inspiration. What message does each of the cards have for you?

Smoke or vape your weed and blow the smoke over your tarot or oracle cards (or use the smoke from cannabis incense) as you shuffle them, focusing on your desire for inspiration.

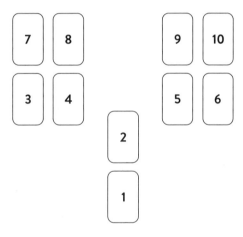

Card 1. Yourself in the current situation.

Card 2. What's blocking you.

Cards 3–10. Each holds a message of inspiration.

Document your drawn cards and their meanings in your journal. Explore your reading in meditation.

APRIL 15
SOULFUL SEARCHING

Get high, meditate, and then journal about how you cope (or don't) with loss. What patterns do you follow? How can you break these patterns and what new, healthier ones can you set for yourself? What good coping strategies do you follow?

APRIL 16
SACRED SMOKE

While mullein is a great medicine for sore throats and lung congestion, it is also used for protection and spirit communication.

Introduce yourself to mullein by using it on its own several times first, exploring it with all your senses. How does it look? Smell? Feel? Taste? You may either smoke it or make a tealike infusion by soaking the leaves in hot water to drink.

How does it affect you? What do you feel when using it? How long does it take to feel the effects? How long do the effects last?

Evaluate and learn how mullein works with your body and mind. Document this information in your Book of Shadows.

Once you become familiar with this herb, combine it with cannabis and again explore the effects, being sure to document your results. This herb can be combined with others to create blends.

APRIL 17
KITCHEN WITCHERY

To draw in or enhance the love in your life, combine the following ingredients in a pot of water to simmer throughout the day.

You will need:

- 1 tablespoon chamomile buds (dried or fresh)
- ¼ cup clover buds (dried or fresh)
- 1 tablespoon jasmine flowers (dried or fresh)
- 1 tablespoon lavender buds (dried or fresh)
- 9 strawberries (dried or fresh)
- 9 raspberries (dried or fresh)
- Pinch of cannabis (dried or fresh)

As you prepare the ingredients and add them to the pot, pour intention into your work. Focus on the type of love you want to welcome into or enhance in your life.

Keep the pot on a low flame on a back burner. Stir the pot nine times clockwise once every hour throughout the day.

Each time you stir the pot, say:

> *Fire, water, earth, and air,*
> *My magic has a little flare.*
> *Fruits from the earth simmer here.*
> *Draw the love I seek near.*

Add more water as needed to replenish what has evaporated. At the end of the day, pour the remains outside on the ground near a tree or under a bush. Return the plant material to the earth it came from. Add this recipe to your BOS and record your own experience with it.

APRIL 18
DELIGHTFUL DABBLING

Charge your weed with rose quartz to infuse it with energies for love, affection, nurturing, and self-love.

For a quick infusion, hold your weed (or other cannabis product) in your nondominant hand with your rose quartz

in your dominant hand. Move the crystal all over and around
the weed and say:

> *Send your energies from here to there,*
> *Infuse this [weed, gummy, THC, etc.]*
> *With affectionate care.*
> *Fill it with love,*
> *To nurture my soul,*
> *Blessed with the power,*
> *To keep my heart whole.*

For a deeper charge, dedicate a small box, chest, or other
type of container where you can charge your cannabis by
placing it, along with a rose quartz, inside.

APRIL 19
ETHEREAL ESSENCES

Research the different correspondences and uses associated
with lime and add a supply to your witch's cupboard. Add
the information you find to your BOS. Dried lime peel can
be crushed and smoked, combined with cannabis, or made
into a tea. Meet the essence of lime in the following meditative practice.

Get into an elevated high and comfortable position with
a small container of dried lime peel, a bottle of lime oil, or
incense lit and placed in front of you.

Close your eyes and take several deep breaths. Allow your mind to settle and focus. When you are ready, pick up the lime and hold it about four inches away from your nose. Inhale the scent, breathing deeply. If it's not too overpowering for you, move it closer. Some people have sensitivities, so don't feel you have to move it directly under your nose. Oils are very potent and do not need to be moved as close.

How does this scent make you feel? Is it pleasing? Irritating? Relaxing? Exciting? Powerful? Meditate on the feelings it evokes in you.

Journal about your experience. If you feel the need to clear the scent from your nose, sniff coffee beans or grounds to help neutralize the scent.

APRIL 20
MAGICAL MUSICAL MOVEMENT

Today is a day to truly celebrate cannabis. Do so by creating your own playlist. Do you prefer the celebratory excitement of a sativa or the dreamy peacefulness of an indica? Perhaps you like to mix it up with a hybrid? Design this playlist to use today and whenever you want to honor your connection with weed. Get high and put your playlist to use!

APRIL 21
VIBING

Your body consists of energy organs and an energetic field. These are often referred to as *chakras* and your *aura*, respectively. The chakras send and receive energy through the auric field.

You can transform energy by filling it with focused intention and sending it back into the universe. You can filter and infuse energy to rerelease it with a new intention. This is where magic comes from. Get high, meditate on this process, and journal about your experience.

APRIL 22
DELIGHTFUL DABBLING

When creating this spell jar to attract love, remember that free will is real. Do not attempt to cast a love spell on a specific person to bring them to you. That is magical manipulation. Instead, focus on the qualities you are looking for in the type of love you want to attract into your life. This does not have to be romantic love either; it is whatever type of love you would like—platonic love, the love of friends, familial love. Focus on the concept of the love you seek, not a physical person.

You will need:

- Glass jar with lid or corked vial
- Dragon's blood (resin or powdered incense)
- Gold flakes (for cake decorating)
- Silver flakes (for cake decorating)
- Chamomile (dried)
- Clover (dried)
- Hibiscus (dried)
- Jasmine (dried)
- Lavender (dried)
- Rose petals (dried)
- Cannabis (dried)
- Lapis lazuli chips
- Moonstone chips
- Quartz chips
- Rose quartz chips
- Pink sealing wax
- Enough red twine to wrap around the top of your jar and tie on a charm
- Heart-shaped charm

Smoke your weed (or use another consumption method, allowing time for edibles to take effect).

Place each ingredient into your chosen jar (or mix them in a bowl and then transfer them to your jar), focusing on each one's energy along with your intention. Visualize a bright pink bubble of light being created around you as you build and bless your jar. This light is a beacon to show love where to find you.

As you work with each ingredient, say:

I call upon the energies of [ingredient name],
Bless me and bring the love I desire into my life.

Take a hit (or deep, centered, intention-filled breath if you do not smoke or vape) and use your exhalation to gently blow your hopes and desires into your jar.

Close the top of the jar and cover it with the melted sealing wax. Wrap the red string around the jar top and attach the heart charm. When finished, say:

Combined together and sealed tight,
Work your magic with my light.
Draw the love I desire near,
I focus and send—my intentions clear.

Place the jar in a prominent location in your home or carry it and your bubble of light with you.

APRIL 23
RECLAIMING THE SHADOW

Get into a high meditative state and connect with your higher self. Reflect on what your friends and family would say about you in a positive recommendation. Which of your qualities would they highlight? What do these qualities say about the image you project to others? Journal about your experience.

APRIL 24
DANK DIVINATION

Use this divination session to interpret messages through smoke.

You will need:

- 2 black candles
- Lighter
- Obsidian stone
- Cannabis incense (optional for nonsmokers)

In a dark or dimly lit room, light two black candles and place them in front of you about ten inches apart. Place an obsidian stone between them.

Smoke or vape your weed, and as you exhale, gently blow the smoke over the obsidian and in between the two candles while opening your mind to receiving images in the smoke. (You may also use the smoke from cannabis incense. If you don't smoke, get high first in your normal manner.)

Record your experience in your Book of Shadows along with any information you obtain through research on smoke scrying.

APRIL 25
MEDITATION MOJO

Settle into a high, meditative state and position. Focus on the concept of love in its various incarnations. What is your definition of love? What does love entail? How does love play a role in your spiritual life? How does your spiritual life play a role in your loving relationships?

APRIL 26
HERBAL BLENDS

Add this nurturing self-love blend to your shadow work or self-care routine.

You will need:

- Motherwort (dried)
- Damiana (dried)
- Sacred lotus petals (dried)
- Rose petals (dried)
- Bergamot (dried)

Combine equal amounts of herbs, then grind them together and combine with your weed in a one-to-one ratio. This blend can either be smoked or infused into tea.

Focus on the self-love and nurturing care you desire as you combine and grind your herbs together, infusing the blend with your intention and energy.

Add this recipe, how it feels, and your results to your Book of Shadows. If you desire, adjust ratios for flavor.

APRIL 27
FIND YOUR WILD

Connect to the night sky with a good high. You do not have to see the stars with your physical eyes if you picture them in your mind's eye. A galaxy map can show you where you are in relation to constellations and the moon to help you get your bearings and give you images to visualize.

Stand outside in the dark with your face to the sky. Either stare into space, taking in everything you can see—the stars, the moon, even satellites and airplanes cutting across the sky—or if it is too cloudy or your view is disrupted by light pollution, picture them in your mind. The energies of air and celestial bodies are all around you. How do these energies feel to you? How do you differentiate them from one another? How can you best utilize them? Add this information to your BOS.

This exercise will be done monthly throughout the year because as the night sky changes, the energies you feel will also change.

APRIL 28
MAGICAL MUSICAL MOVEMENT

Start a playlist of empowering songs. This playlist can be used when you want to raise energy for spellwork, to help focus your attention on empowerment, or simply as background music while you do any type of empowerment spell prep work or journal writing.

Try out your playlist by choosing a few songs to move to in whatever type of dance you like to raise energy. Get yourself to a good, elevated, happy high (sativa or a hybrid recommended).

Focus on what empowerment feels like to you. Visualize the qualities you want to harness. Raise your energy and release it into the universe to bring these qualities to you.

Try listening to your playlist motionless with your eyes closed or with a blindfold to block out other distractions. Use headphones if possible. Does it create the energy and emotion you desired? Let the music motivate you.

APRIL 29
INTRIGUING INCANTATIONS

The absence of love hurts. Love keeps us safe; love keeps us content. Whether it be platonic, familial, romantic, or self-love, love is an important part of a happy, healthy life.

Take a hit, focus on the type of love you want to attract or mend in your life, and say:

> *Bring love into my life*
> *When it is lacking, I feel the strife.*
> *Open my heart to love that is true,*
> *For it is the cure to what makes me blue.*

Use this chant on its own or in conjunction with other spellwork.

APRIL 30
SOULFUL SEARCHING

How did your month go? What types of love did you work with over this past month? How were you able to connect with and tap into the natural energies of vibrancy, life, and rebirth?

Meditate and journal on your overall experiences and how they contributed to your practice, spirituality, or both.

May

In this second month of spring, you will still work with some of the same energies as last month. Nature is coming alive all around you. Romance and love are in the air. This month, while you will still work with the energies of love, throw a bit of romance in with it.

The following are all aspects of romance:

- Adventure
- Charm
- Excitement
- Fantasy
- Fascination
- Flight of fancy

- Glamour
- Mystery
- Venture

Don't limit yourself to only one definition!

May Supply List

May 2

6×6-inch square piece of red material

Small piece of rose quartz

Essential oil, dried herb, or resin: heather, jasmine, rose, lavender, lovage, sandalwood

Cannabis flower (dried)

6 inches of gold ribbon

Cannabis incense (optional for nonsmokers)

May 5

Glass jar(s) with lid(s) or corked vial(s)

Maple (crushed dried leaves of seed pods: "helicopters." If your jar is large enough, you can put in a whole seed pod.)

Dried: daisy petals, dill, feverfew, lilac, marjoram, mugwort, sage, thyme, cannabis

Bloodstone chips

Mauve sealing wax

Enough white twine to wrap around the top of
your jar and tie on a charm

Heart-shaped charm(s) (or you can use your
zodiac signs)

May 8

Glass jar with lid or corked vial

Dried: lavender, lemon balm, heather, sacred lotus
petals, motherwort, damiana, cannabis (dried)

Amber chips

Aventurine chips

Citrine chips

Purple sealing wax

Enough silver twine to wrap around the top of
your jar and tie on a charm

Heart-shaped charm

May 14

Cannabis incense (optional for nonsmokers)

May 16

Blue vervain

May 17

Dried or fresh: heather buds, jasmine buds, lavender
buds, rose petals, cannabis

May 18

Glass jar with lid or corked vial

Dried: bergamot, chamomile, dandelion leaves,
mustard seed, cannabis

Cinnamon (ground or broken pieces of a stick)

Green jasper chips

Paper (optional)

Writing instrument (optional)

Green sealing wax

Enough gold twine to wrap around the top of
your jar and tie on a charm

Money charm

May 19

Basil

May 20

Rosebuds

Lavender buds

Jasmine buds

Tea strainer or cheesecloth bag

THC (either ground flower or oil extract)

Champagne, white wine, sparkling white grape juice, or white grape juice

Honey

May 24

2 black candles

Lighter

Crystal ball

Cannabis incense (optional for nonsmokers)

May 26

Dried: hops, hibiscus, damiana, jasmine, lavender, pink rose petals

MAY 1
LIT LITERATURE

Turn your focus to researching as many different gods as you can with brief introductions to them. Do not focus on books dedicated to an individual god; instead, look for titles that cover at least a couple dozen. Take note of any specific gods who catch your attention for further research later.

No matter where you shop for books, use the keywords "gods" or "books on gods" in your search to find titles of interest.

MAY 2
TEMPTING TALISMAN

Build this talisman to draw romance into your life while focusing on what your definition of romance means to you. What aspect of romance do you want to bring into or enhance in your life?

Try to use a mix of oils and dried ingredients if available to you. Use a pinch of dried ingredients and a drop or two of oils.

You will need:

- 6 × 6-inch square of red material
- Small piece of rose quartz
- Heather (essential oil, dried herb, or resin)
- Jasmine (essential oil, dried herb, or resin)
- Rose (essential oil, dried herb, or resin)
- Lavender (essential oil, dried herb, or resin)
- Lovage (essential oil, dried herb, or resin)

- Sandalwood (essential oil, dried herb, or resin)
- Cannabis flower (dried)
- 6 inches of gold ribbon
- Cannabis incense (optional for nonsmokers)

Smoke your weed (or use another consumption method) while you assemble your ingredients and create this talisman. If you have room to work at your altar, do so, or create another sacred space where you have room and are comfortable.

Lay the red square on your altar or other stable location. Begin with the largest ingredients you are working with, most likely your piece of rose quartz in this instance. Add it to the center of the material.

Next, add any smaller dried herbs (including your flower), resins, or chips. Top these off with three drops of any essential oils you use. Drip them onto a dried herb or piece of wood so they soak into those instead of just the material.

Remember to focus on your vision of romance as you work. What do you want to draw to you? Envision your life with those aspects of romance fulfilled. What does it look like? How does it feel? Pour those feelings and energies into your talisman.

When you are done filling it, bunch the material up into a pouch and wrap the gold ribbon around the neck three times before knotting it off. As you wrap and tie the ribbon, say:

What I command, make it be.
I bid these energies to work with me.
What I wish,
So mote it be.

Take a hit and release your intention and exhale your smoke all over the pouch. (You may also use the smoke from cannabis incense along with your own breath.)

Carry this talisman throughout the month to keep this bubble of magnetic energy with you.

MAY 3
ASTROLOGICAL HOUSES

Research the meaning of the astrological fifth house and explore the role it plays in your life within your own chart. The fifth house represents your creativity. Record the information you learn and how it relates to your sign and yourself in your Book of Shadows or a journal.

MAY 4
VIBING

"The Force is what gives a Jedi his power. It's an energy field created by all living things. It surrounds us and penetrates us.

It binds the galaxy together." —Obi-Wan Kenobi, *Stars Wars: Episode IV—A New Hope.*

How a witch uses the energies created by living things (such as plants!) is remarkably similar to how a Jedi uses the Force. Get high and celebrate International Star Wars Day (maybe with some X-Wing, Skywalker, or Boba Fett!) by either meditating about, or using, the Force.

May the Force be with you, always.

MAY 5
DELIGHTFUL DABBLING

This spell is designed to celebrate the love already in your life. You have a few options available to you for how to proceed depending on what works best for your situation. You may create one jar, which will encompass the love of two or more people (for example, to celebrate family love, you may want one large jar in which each family member adds ingredients), or you may create multiple jars with one for each person. You might want to create your own celebration of love jar from combined supplies, or you and a partner can create jars for each other—whatever works best for your situation.

You will need:

- Glass jar(s) with lid or corked vial(s)
- Maple (crushed dried leaves of seed pods: "helicopters." If your jar is large enough, you can put in a whole seed pod.)
- Daisy petals (dried)
- Dill (dried)
- Feverfew (dried)
- Lilac (dried)
- Marjoram (dried)
- Mugwort (dried)
- Sage (dried)
- Thyme (dried)
- Cannabis (dried)
- Bloodstone chips
- Mauve sealing wax
- Enough white twine to wrap around the top of your jar and tie on a charm
- Heart-shaped charm(s) (or you can use your zodiac signs)

Smoke your weed (or use another consumption method, allowing time for edibles to take effect).

Place each ingredient into your chosen jar, layering them on top of each other and focusing on each one's energy along with your intention. Keep in mind the love you are celebrating as you build and bless your jar. If you are working with someone, take turns if you want, or work with each ingredient together.

As you do, say:

[I or we] call upon the energies of [ingredient name],
Come to [me or us] and empower [my or our] work.

Take a hit (or deep, centered, intention-filled breath if you do not smoke or vape) and use your exhalation to gently blow an expression of your love into your jar.

Close the top of the jar and cover it with the melted sealing wax. Wrap the string around the jar top and attach the charm(s). When finished, say:

[I or we] honor and cherish the love we share,
Our energies enhanced because we care.
Combined together, energies entwined.
Each layer supported,
Our ties do bind.

Display your jar in a prominent location where its energy will fill your home.

MAY 6
CERRIDWEN'S CAULDRON

Maiden. Mother. Crone. Huntress. Mystic. Sage. Muse. Wild Woman. Healer. Seductress. Warrioress. The various aspects of the divine feminine are represented through different goddess archetypes. Research goddess archetypes. Which type(s) do you currently connect with and how?

MAY 7
LIFTED PERSPECTIVE

Get into a comfortable position and a meditative high. Whether an eagle or hummingbird, imagine yourself as a bird flying high above an area you know well. Use a 3D map program such as Google Earth if you need help to visualize what it should look like. Soar on the wind as you observe everything below you. Where do you go and what do you see?

MAY 8
DELIGHTFUL DABBLING

Emotional healing begins when you are willing to look through your past (whether recent or ancient!) and confront old heartaches and wounds. As you create this spell jar to assist in healing your emotional health, focus on opening yourself to the healing process.

You will need:

- Glass jar with lid or corked vial
- Lavender (dried)
- Lemon balm (dried)
- Heather (dried)
- Sacred lotus petals (dried)
- Motherwort (dried)
- Damiana (dried)
- Cannabis (dried)
- Amber chips
- Aventurine chips
- Citrine chips
- Purple sealing wax
- Enough silver twine to wrap around the top of your jar and tie on a charm
- Heart-shaped charm

Smoke your weed (or use another consumption method, allowing time for edibles to take effect).

Place each ingredient into your chosen jar (or mix them in a bowl and then transfer them to your jar), focusing on each one's energy along with your intention. Visualize a protective, supportive, nurturing bubble being created around you as you build and bless your jar.

As you work with each ingredient, say:

I call to the spirit of [ingredient name],
I summon your energies to support my journey.

Take a hit (or deep, centered, intention-filled breath if you do not smoke or vape) and use your exhalation to gently blow your hopes and objectives into your jar.

Close the top of the jar and cover it with the melted sealing wax. Wrap the string around the jar top and attach the charm. When finished, say:

Wounds within I need to heal,
Magic to assist contained in this seal.
Give me strength to face my past
And courage to make change that lasts
Protect my heart,
Nurture my soul,
Working together to make myself whole.

When doing shadow work, therapeutic exercises, or even having a good cry, hold on to your jar for magical support. Repeat the above chant to activate its use.

MAY 9
FIND YOUR WILD

Find a place outside where you can connect with plant life, whether it be a tree, flowers, a patch of grass, or even a potted fern on a balcony. Get high and focus on the plant. Observe every detail you can about it. How does it smell? How does it feel? If you know it's safe to do so, you can taste it. What vibes does your chosen plant give you?

MAY 10
EMBRACING THE ELEMENTS

Crossroads and crossroads dirt are used in road opening (obstacle removing) spells, journeys to the underworld, or as an offering.

Find or make a crossroads you can use to harvest dirt from or for when you need a place for things to be buried. The crossroads needs to be outside in a location where small things can be buried and must include some sort of intersection. Can you design a crossroads on your own property in your yard or garden? Design one yourself with mowing patterns or even using a stick to draw an intersection in mud. Brainstorm and list your available crossroads in your Book of Shadows.

MAY 11
GROWING WITH THE GREEN MAN

Get high and find a patch of grass you can lay tummy down on. You don't need to stick your face in the dirt, so find a comfortable position in which you can actively look down into the grass and the soil it grows from.

Observe your selected spot for several minutes using as many of your physical senses as possible. No, you don't need to taste the grass or dirt, but you can taste the air right above them. How do the grass and dirt feel to the touch? What do you see? Any little critters looking back at you? What do you hear?

Set your physical observations aside. Close your eyes and *feel* instead. Connect with these energies. Journal about your experience.

MAY 12
SUPERNATURAL SENSES

Clairsentience, meaning clear sensing, can be described as "when you know, you know," though you don't know how or why you know. You know? It's when you clearly know something, though you didn't learn it through any conscious means. It may come on as sudden knowledge, you discover it was "always there," or sometimes it feels like a swift kick in the gut and you simply *know*. This can also be thought of as a strong intuition or gut instinct beyond the norm.

Cannabis helps to lower the walls and make the connection so clairsentience can be easier to access, particularly when in a deeply meditative state. Open your higher self to sensing messages from your gut, Spirit, or the spirit world.

Get high and think about times you listened to your intuition. Is your intuition usually right on or way off? How do you know when the information you receive is a form of clairsentience? What physical reactions does your body have? What energy shifts can you detect? How does it *feel* for you when this strong intuition hits?

Document your experiences in your BOS and be sure to update it as new events occur. If you are interested in this, be sure to add this topic to your research list to gather more information.

MAY 13
RECLAIMING THE SHADOW

Meet your higher self in a meditative state. Choose to revisit a time of confusion when you felt deceived or betrayed. What was the catalyst for your feelings? How did you express your feelings at the time? If you could express them differently now, would you? And if so, how? What support, if any, did you receive?

Give yourself what you needed but didn't receive. Journal about your experience.

MAY 14
DANK DIVINATION

Smoke or vape your weed and blow the smoke over your tarot or oracle cards as you shuffle them, focusing on receiving a message from your higher self. (You may also use the smoke of cannabis incense.)

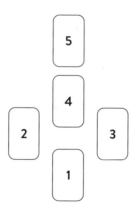

Card 1. My current situation.

Card 2. Where I have been distracted.

Card 3. What I've been missing.

Card 4. How cards 2 and 3 affect me.

Card 5. Message from my higher self.

Document your drawn cards and their meanings in your journal. Explore your reading in meditation.

MAY 15
VIBING

Get into a comfortable high and position. Then, light a candle (any candle) in front of you. Focus on the edges and tip of the flame. Find what resembles an aura around the flame. This is visible yet hard-to-see energy. How far around the flame can you see this energy field? Carefully place your palm or fingers near the flame but not close enough to burn. Can you feel the energy field? Most energies we work with are more difficult to see. We can use this example of what energy looks like to help visualize invisible energies. Journal about your experience.

MAY 16
SACRED SMOKE

Blue vervain is a powerful magical herb. It assists in spirit communication, lucid dreaming, and astral projection. It is also great for relieving anxiety and calming the body and mind. When combined with an indica strain, it boosts the traits of both.

Introduce yourself to blue vervain by using it on its own several times first, exploring it with all your senses. How does it look? Smell? Feel? Taste? You may either smoke it or make a tealike infusion by soaking the leaves in hot water to drink.

How does it affect you? What do you feel when using it? How long does it take to feel the effects? How long do the effects last?

Evaluate and learn how blue vervain works with your body and mind. Document this information in your Book of Shadows.

Once you become familiar with this herb, combine it with cannabis and again explore the effects, being sure to document your results. This herb can be combined with others to create blends.

MAY 17
KITCHEN WITCHERY

To draw in or enhance the romance in your life, combine the following ingredients in a pot of water to simmer throughout the day.

You will need:

- ¼ cup heather buds (dried or fresh)
- ¼ cup jasmine buds (dried or fresh)
- ¼ cup lavender buds (dried or fresh)
- ¼ cup rose petals (dried or fresh)
- Pinch of cannabis (dried or fresh)

As you prepare the ingredients and add them to the pot, pour intention into your work. Focus on the romance you want to bring into your life.

Keep the pot on a low flame on a back burner. Stir the pot nine times clockwise once every hour throughout the day.

Each time you stir the pot, say:

Fire, water, earth, and air,
My magic has a little flare.
Fruits from the earth simmer here.
Romance in my life shall appear.

Add more water as needed to replenish what has evaporated. At the end of the day, pour the remains outside on the ground near a tree or under a bush. Return the plant material to the earth it came from. Add this recipe to your BOS and record your own experience with it.

MAY 18
DELIGHTFUL DABBLING

Add to your funds with this spell jar to attract money to your wallet.

You will need:

- Glass jar with lid or corked vial
- Bergamot (dried)
- Chamomile (dried)
- Dandelion leaves (dried)
- Mustard seed (dried)
- Cannabis (dried)
- Cinnamon (ground or broken pieces of a stick)
- Green jasper chips
- Paper (optional)
- Writing instrument (optional)
- Green sealing wax

- Enough gold twine to wrap around the top of your jar and tie on a charm
- Money charm

Smoke your weed (or use another consumption method, allowing time for edibles to take effect).

Place each ingredient into your chosen jar (or mix them in a bowl and then transfer them to your jar), focusing on each one's energy along with your intention. Visualize the money you need and what it is for as you build and bless your jar.

As you work with each ingredient, say:

I call upon the energies of [ingredient name],
Help draw the money I need to me.

If you are looking for a specific amount for a specific reason, write it on a piece of paper and place it in the jar.

Take a hit (or deep, centered, intention-filled breath if you do not smoke or vape) and use your exhalation to gently blow your hopes and objectives into your jar.

Close the top of the jar and cover it with the melted sealing wax. Wrap the string around the jar top and attach the charm. When finished, say:

Nickels, dimes, and quarters,
Every cent adds up.
Fives, tens, twenties,

Overfilling my cup.
Money, money, money,
Bring a little here.
Money, money, money,
Need a little there.
Money, money, money,
Help me obtain what's right.
Money, money, money,
I call you with my might.

Carry your jar or vial with you or place it in a prominent place in your home. Keep your wallet or checkbook close by it when you can.

MAY 19
ETHEREAL ESSENCES

Research the different correspondences and uses associated with basil and add a supply to your witch's cupboard. Add the information you find to your BOS. Dried basil can be smoked, combined with cannabis, or made into a tea. Meet the essence of basil in the following meditative practice.

Get into an elevated high and comfortable position with a small container of dried basil, a bottle of basil oil, or incense lit and placed in front of you.

Close your eyes and take several deep breaths. Allow your mind to settle and focus. When you are ready, pick up the basil and hold it about four inches away from your nose. Inhale the scent, breathing deeply. If it's not too overpowering for you, move it closer. Some people have sensitivities, so don't feel you have to move it directly under your nose. Oils are very potent and do not need to be moved as close.

How does this scent make you feel? Is it pleasing? Irritating? Relaxing? Exciting? Powerful? Meditate on the feelings it evokes in you.

Journal about your experience. If you feel the need to clear the scent from your nose, sniff coffee beans or grounds to help neutralize the scent.

MAY 20
HERBAL INFUSIONS

Create this infusion for a sense of adventurous romance. This recipe works for either an alcoholic or a nonalcoholic drink. It's a light, flowery drink with a hint of honey sweetness.

You will need:

- Rosebuds
- Lavender buds
- Jasmine buds
- Tea strainer or cheesecloth bag

- THC (either ground flower or oil extract)
- Champagne, white wine, sparkling white grape juice, or white grape juice
- Honey

Mix equal parts of the flower buds and add to a tea strainer or cheesecloth bag to infuse in your chosen drink. If you are using ground cannabis, be sure it is decarboxylated first, and use a pinch for each drink. Add the ground cannabis to the strainer or cheesecloth. Concentrated oil or syrup can be added after the infusion.

You will want to use 1 teaspoon of each flower for each drink. For example, if you are making a single drink, you will have a total of three teaspoons. If you are infusing a full wine or champagne bottle, these are considered four drinks, so you will need four teaspoons of each flower for a total of twelve teaspoons. Because of the quantity, you will need a good airtight container to infuse the champagne or wine in. Pour the liquid slowly at a slight angle into a container large enough to hold it and the flower buds, leaving as little air space as possible to help keep it from going flat. Chill for three to four hours.

A teaspoon of honey (may also be THC infused) can be stirred into each drink when served. Before serving the drink, squirt the honey around the top inside of the glass. It will spread its sweetness as it slides down.

MAY 21
VIBING

Vibrations may be low and slow or high and fast. Think back to your high school chemistry class for a great analogy of how vibrations work.

Ice is a solid. It has slow and low vibrations. When ice melts and it becomes water, its vibrations are faster and higher. If you heat water, it becomes steam, which vibrates even higher and faster.

Some days you may feel like a block of ice. Your vibrations are low and slow. Most days you probably feel more like water moving along at a steady pace, and other times, when you have a profound spiritual moment or high, you are steam.

When you feel like ice, what can you do to melt yourself into water? Get high and meditate on this process and journal about your experience.

MAY 22
SOULFUL SEARCHING

What level of confidence do you have in yourself as a witch? Explain the positive and negatives of why you feel this way. What do you wish to improve? Where do your interests lie?

Document this information in your Book of Shadows. Leave space to update it over the years to see how your confidence, and interests, grow.

MAY 23
RECLAIMING THE SHADOW

Consume your cannabis and meet with your higher self in a deep meditative state. Recall various times when you felt your heart was broken. Think about the events and behaviors that led to these moments. What common themes do you find? What have you learned about yourself from these heartbreaks? Journal about your experience.

MAY 24
DANK DIVINATION

Use this divination session to interpret messages through a crystal ball.

You will need:

- 2 black candles
- Lighter
- Crystal ball
- Cannabis incense (optional for nonsmokers)

In a dark or dimly lit room, light two black candles and place them in front of you about ten inches apart. Place your crystal ball between them.

Smoke or vape your weed, and as you exhale, gently blow the smoke over the crystal ball and in between the two candles while opening your mind to receiving images through the smoke. (You may also blow the smoke from cannabis incense and get high with another consumption method.)

Record your experience in your Book of Shadows along with any information you obtain through research on using a crystal ball.

MAY 25
MEDITATION MOJO

Get high and settle into a meditative state and position. Conjure a vision of your most romantic dream date. Where do you go? What do you do? Whom do you go with? The only limits are your imagination.

MAY 26
HERBAL BLENDS

Set the mood for a little romance with this blend.

You will need:

- Hops (dried)

- Hibiscus (dried)

- Damiana (dried)

- Jasmine (dried)

- Lavender (dried)

- Pink rose petals (dried)

Start by combining equal parts of the herbs and grind together. Blend with ground bud in a one-to-one ratio. This blend can be smoked or brewed into tea.

Use this blend on its own for a boost or to accompany your romance-themed spellwork. Focus on the romance you are seeking as you combine and grind your herbs together, infusing the blend with your intention and energy.

Add this recipe, how it feels, and your results to your Book of Shadows. If you desire, adjust ratios for flavor.

MAY 27
FIND YOUR WILD

Connect to the night sky with a good high. You do not have to see the stars with your physical eyes if you picture them in your mind's eye. A galaxy map can show you where you are in relation to constellations and the moon to help you get your bearings and give you images to visualize.

Stand outside in the dark with your face to the sky. Either stare into space, taking in everything you can see—the stars, the moon, even satellites and airplanes cutting across the sky—or if it is too cloudy or your view is disrupted by light pollution, picture them in your mind. The energies of air and celestial bodies are all around you. How do these energies feel to you? How do you differentiate them from one another? How can you best utilize them? Add this information to your BOS.

This exercise will be done monthly throughout the year because as the night sky changes, the energies you feel will also change.

MAY 28
MAGICAL MUSICAL MOVEMENT

Start a playlist of romance-themed songs. This playlist can be used when you want to raise energy for spellwork, to create a romantic setting, or simply as background music while you do any type of romance spellwork prep.

Try out your playlist by getting high and choosing a few songs to move to in whatever type of dance you like to raise energy. Get yourself to a good, elevated, happy high. Raise your energy and release it into the universe to bring these qualities to you.

Try listening to your playlist motionless with your eyes closed or with a blindfold to block out other distractions.

Use headphones if possible. Does it create the energy, environment, and emotion you desired?

MAY 29
INTRIGUING INCANTATIONS

Life can be dull and boring or exciting and adventurous. And of course, a bit of each. When you need to draw a little romance into your life, light up and repeat this chant:

> *Romance for life, exciting and mysterious,*
> *Sensual and flirty—a heartbeat delirious.*
> *Adventure and fun; life be enhanced,*
> *Spice up my life with fate and chance.*

Use this chant on its own or add it to other spellwork.

MAY 30
DELIGHTFUL DABBLING

Pick a strain today that makes you giggly. Give yourself a good high and let yourself laugh off stress, anxiety, and other negative feelings. Allow laughter to wash over you. When you are good and stoned, it gets difficult to stop laughing once you get going, so go as long as you can. Replenish and refresh yourself with a good ole long, silly giggle.

Keep a running list in your Book of Shadows of strains that have this effect on you so you'll know your go-to when needed. Feel free to journal about your experience, perhaps with before and after entries to compare how you feel.

MAY 31
SOULFUL SEARCHING

Reflect on the previous month. What romance did you conjure into your life? How did you connect with the energies of spring? Meditate and journal on your experiences and how they improved your life and added to your practice and spirituality.

June

Summer will soon begin, which is often a busy time for people. The energies in the natural world are healthy, vibrant, and full of growth and life. Summer can be energetic, and chaotic. This month, balance this burst with working on ways to add and encourage peace in your life.

June Supply List
June 2

    5 × 5-inch square piece of gray material

    Rose quartz (a stone or a few chips)

    Olive leaf (dried)

Essential oil, dried herb, or resin: magnolia, gardenia, jasmine, lily of the valley

6 inches of silver string

Cannabis incense (optional for nonsmokers)

June 8

Your water charger

Rose

Motherwort

Rose quartz

June 14

Cannabis incense (optional for nonsmokers)

June 16

Wormwood

June 17

Dried or fresh: blue vervain, lavender buds, jasmine buds, lilac flowers, white lily, rose petals, violets, cannabis

June 18

Amethyst

June 19

Ylang-ylang

June 20

Your water charger

Chamomile

Lavender

Amethyst

June 22

Ground cannabis

June 24

2 black candles

Lighter

Black mirror

Cannabis incense (optional for nonsmokers)

June 26

Dried: hops, lavender, catnip, blue vervain, lemon
balm, tulsi, rose, chamomile

JUNE 1
LIT LITERATURE

Cannabis and hemp have lived quite different histories else-where in the world when compared to their American past. Honored and accepted in many other countries, it was used to control immigrants to the United States. This month, gain knowledge by learning what you can from other cultures.

No matter where you shop for books, use the keywords "world history cannabis" in your search to find titles of interest.

JUNE 2
TEMPTING TALISMAN

Gather natural energies of peace to store in this talisman to use when you need a moment of calm. Try to use a mix of oils and dried ingredients if available to you. Use a pinch of dried ingredients and a drop or two of oils.

You will need:

- 5 × 5-inch square piece of gray material

- Rose quartz (a stone or a few chips)

- Olive leaf (dried)

- Magnolia (essential oil, dried herb, or resin)

- Gardenia (essential oil, dried herb, or resin)

- Jasmine (essential oil, dried herb, or resin)

- Lily of the valley (essential oil, dried herb, or resin)

- 6 inches of silver string

- Cannabis incense (optional for nonsmokers)

Smoke your weed (or use another consumption method) while you assemble your ingredients and create this talisman. If you have room to work at your altar, do so, or create another sacred space where you have room and are comfortable.

Lay the gray square on your altar or other stable location. Begin with the largest ingredients you are working with, most likely your piece of rose quartz in this instance. Add it to the center of the material.

Next, add any smaller dried herbs or flowers. Top these off with one drop of any essential oils you use. Drip them onto a dried herb or flower so they soak into those instead of the material.

Remember to focus on your vision of peace as you work. What does it look like? How does it feel? Pour those feelings and energies into your talisman.

When you are done filling it, bunch the material up into a pouch and wrap the ribbon around the neck three times before knotting it off.

Use this chant to help guide your intentions and work:

Magic swirling through the air,
Energies of peace—gather here.
I pluck and pull each one to save,
To store and use when peace I crave.

Take a hit and release your intention and exhale your smoke all over the pouch. (You may also use the smoke from cannabis incense along with your own breath.)

Store your talisman on your altar or in another magical, safe space. Hold it to your heart, accompanied by deep breathing, when you need to use its stored energy.

JUNE 3
SOULFUL SEARCHING

How do you stifle your authentic self? How do you deny your authentic self a voice? What do you stop yourself from doing or saying? Why do you hold back?

Get high and connect with your higher self or power in a deep meditative state and listen to what they have to say. Journal about your experience.

JUNE 4
ASTROLOGICAL HOUSES

Research the meaning of the astrological sixth house and explore the role it plays in your life within your own chart. The sixth house represents your health. Record the information you learn and how it relates to your sign and yourself in your Book of Shadows or a journal.

JUNE 5
MEDITATION MOJO

Get high and relax. Place your left hand on your stomach and your right hand on your heart. Feel both your chest and your stomach rise and fall with each breath. Focus deeply on this breath. Inhale through your nose and breathe out through your mouth. After several breaths, think to yourself, "I am at peace" on each exhale. Continue for as long as you like and experience this peace you create and give to yourself.

JUNE 6
CERRIDWEN'S CAULDRON

Artist. Dark Knight. Director. Hunter. King. Lover. Poet. Priest. Sage. Warrior. The various aspects of the masculine are represented through different god archetypes. Research god archetypes. Which type(s) do you currently connect with and how?

JUNE 7
LIFTED PERSPECTIVE

Use this exercise on uncompleted goals for a new perspective on achieving them.

Get high and create a list of your uncompleted goals, listing the reason(s) why each goal has not yet been completed. For example: "I want to buy a new car, but I can't afford it." Do not read beyond this sentence until your list of goals and reasons are complete.

Now go back through your list, replacing the word "but" with the word "and," and reread your statements. Let this new perspective help you reevaluate your goals.

JUNE 8
DELIGHTFUL DABBLING

Using your water charger, combine water and earth together in this bong water herbal infusion for self-love.

You will need:

- Your water charger
- Rose
- Motherwort
- Rose quartz

You may either add rose and motherwort to the water to steep or place the plant matter with the rose quartz separate from your water but in close proximity. Use this water in your bong for a comforting boost of self-love.

JUNE 9
FIND YOUR WILD

Find a place outside where you can get high and safely observe a type of animal life—a bird, a squirrel, your own pet, farm animals, geckos, or any type of animal that is available to you. Get high and focus on your chosen animal. Observe every detail you can about it and its actions. What does the animal look like? Sound like? Smell like? Is it playful? Territorial? Is it working? What vibes does this animal give you?

JUNE 10
EMBRACING THE ELEMENTS

Working with water from natural water sources allows you to incorporate the energies from those water sources into your workings. Do you live near a vast ocean with powerful waves? This water represents intense forces. Is there a small bubbling brook you can access? This water represents joy and lightheartedness. Even stagnant water from a local bog has magical use.

Use a map, brainstorm, and list your available natural water sources and their corresponding qualities in your Book of Shadows.

JUNE 11
GROWING WITH THE GREEN MAN

Get high and find a tree to observe. Touch the bark and leaves. Smell them. Listen to the leaves (or needles) in the breeze. Watch as the light reflects off them. Look at the tree from different angles. Lie down underneath the branches and look up into it. Try to feel and connect with the tree's spirit or energies. Journal about your experience.

JUNE 12
SUPERNATURAL SENSES

Psychometry is receiving information and impressions through touch. The psychometer holds on to an item and receives information about it and its owner through energy stored in the item.

Cannabis helps to lower the walls and make the connection so psychometry is easier to access, particularly when in a deeply meditative state. Open your higher self to sensing messages from different items. If you have rings from several different people, practice sensing blindfolded which ring belongs to which person. This can be fun to do with a group, where everyone adds items to a bag and then each person pulls an item from the bag to see what they can feel.

Document your experiences in your BOS and be sure to update it as new events occur. If you are interested in this, be sure to add this topic to your research list to gather more information.

JUNE 13
RECLAIMING THE SHADOW

Northern Lights is a popular strain named after the beautiful, ever-changing scientific phenomenon also known as the aurora borealis. These lights are only visible under certain conditions, which occur in relatively few places on earth, meaning to experience their beauty, one must generally seek them out.

Slip into a high and deep meditative state and look to the stars and your higher power or self. What beauty do you need to seek out in your life? What do you need the light to be able to see?

JUNE 14
DANK DIVINATION

Smoke or vape your weed and blow the smoke over your tarot or oracle cards as you shuffle them, focusing on receiving a message from your higher self or power about how to break out of your comfort zone. (You may consume your cannabis in another manner and use the smoke from cannabis incense instead.)

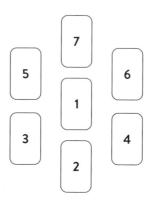

Card 1. My current situation.

Card 2. What grounds me and makes me feel safe in my comfort zone.

Card 3. What holds me back.

Card 4. How do I build or maintain stability while conducting change?

Card 5. What is calling me?

Card 6. Guidance from higher self.

Card 7. What new adventure awaits.

Document your drawn cards and their meanings in your journal. Explore your reading in meditation.

JUNE 15
SOULFUL SEARCHING

Get high, meditate, and then journal about your greatest strengths. How do you use them? How do you waste them? How can you better utilize these talents?

JUNE 16
SACRED SMOKE

Wormwood (of absinthe fame) is an ideal herb for spirit communication, deity work, shadow work, creative exploration, and other types of workings with your higher self. When combined with cannabis, the effects are intensified.

Introduce yourself to wormwood by using it on its own several times first, exploring it with all your senses. How does it look? Smell? Feel? Taste? You may either smoke it or make a tealike infusion by soaking the leaves in hot water to drink.

How does it affect you? What do you feel when using it? How long does it take to feel the effects? How long do the effects last?

Evaluate and learn how wormwood works with your body and mind. Document this information in your Book of Shadows.

Once you become familiar with this herb, combine it with cannabis and again explore the effects, being sure to document your results. This herb can be combined with others to create blends.

JUNE 17
KITCHEN WITCHERY

To draw in and maintain peace in your life, combine the following ingredients in a pot of water to simmer throughout the day.

You will need:

- 1 tablespoon blue vervain (dried or fresh)
- 1 tablespoon lavender buds (dried or fresh)
- 1 tablespoon jasmine buds (dried or fresh)
- 1 tablespoon lilac flowers (dried or fresh)
- 1 whole white lily (dried or fresh)
- 1 tablespoon rose petals (dried or fresh)
- 1 tablespoon violets (dried or fresh)
- Pinch of cannabis (dried or fresh)

As you prepare the ingredients and add them to the pot, pour intention into your work. Focus on your life being calm and at peace in all areas.

Keep the pot on a low flame on a back burner. Stir the pot nine times clockwise, once every hour throughout the day.

Each time you stir the pot, say:

Fire, water, earth, and air,
My magic has a little flare.
Fruits from the earth simmer here.
Peace in my life, I will hold dear.

Add more water as needed to replenish what has evaporated. At the end of the day, pour the remains outside on the ground near a tree or under a bush. Return the plant material to the earth it came from. Add this recipe to your BOS and record your own experience with it.

JUNE 18
DELIGHTFUL DABBLING

Charge your weed with amethyst to infuse it with energies for divination and spiritual and psychic work.

For a quick infusion, hold your weed (or other cannabis product) in your nondominant hand with your amethyst in your dominant hand. Move the amethyst all over and around the weed and say:

Infuse this [weed, gummy, THC, etc.]
With energies true,

Combine together,
Power comes through.
Help open my mind,
And my third eye,
Bring visions to me,
When I am high.

For a deeper charge, dedicate a small box, chest, or other type of container where you can charge your cannabis by placing it, along with an amethyst, inside.

JUNE 19
ETHEREAL ESSENCES

Research the different correspondences and uses associated with ylang-ylang and add a supply to your witch's cupboard. Add the information you find to your BOS. Meet the essence of ylang-ylang in the following meditative practice.

Get into an elevated high and comfortable position with a small container of dried ylang-ylang, a bottle of oil, or incense lit and placed in front of you.

Close your eyes and take several deep breaths. Allow your mind to settle and focus. When you are ready, pick up the ylang-ylang and hold it about four inches away from your nose. Inhale the scent, breathing deeply. If it's not too overpowering for you, move it closer. Some people have sensitivities, so don't feel you have to move it directly under your nose. Oils are very potent and do not need to be moved as close.

How does this scent make you feel? Is it pleasing? Irritating? Relaxing? Exciting? Powerful? Meditate on the feelings it evokes in you.

Journal about your experience. If you feel the need to clear the scent from your nose, sniff coffee beans or grounds to help neutralize the scent.

JUNE 20
HERBAL INFUSIONS

Using your water charger, combine water and earth together in this bong water herbal infusion for inner peace.

You will need:

- Your water charger
- Chamomile
- Lavender
- Amethyst

You may either add the chamomile and lavender to the water to steep or place the plant matter with the amethyst separate from your water but in close proximity. Use this water in your bong (or drink) to help restore inner peace.

JUNE 21
VIBING

Use a blindfold or eye mask and headphones to immerse yourself in the vibrations of binaural music. Experiment with different frequencies and with how high you are. Enjoy vibing with these energies and journal about your experience.

JUNE 22
DELIGHTFUL DABBLING

Use weed to charge and protect stored crystals and tools. Rub a bit of ground bud between your fingers to scatter over your crystals and tools. Say:

> *This is my will to impress,*
> *A sprinkle of weed,*
> *Here to bless.*

Store your tools as you normally would.

JUNE 23
RECLAIMING THE SHADOW

Get into a deep meditative high and connect with your higher self or power.

Answer the questions, What boundaries do I need to set and enforce in my life? With myself? With others?

Listen to what your higher self tells you. Journal about your experience and work on creating boundary-setting statements pertinent to your personal situations.

JUNE 24
DANK DIVINATION

Use this divination session to interpret messages through a black mirror.

You will need:

- 2 black candles
- Lighter
- Black mirror
- Cannabis incense (optional for nonsmokers)

In a dark or dimly lit room, light two black candles and place them in front of you about ten inches apart. Place your black mirror between them.

Smoke or vape your weed, and as you exhale, gently blow the smoke over the mirror and in between the two candles while opening your mind to receiving images. (You may consume your cannabis in a different way and use the smoke from a cannabis incense stick.)

Record your experience in your Book of Shadows along with any information you obtain through research on using a black mirror.

JUNE 25
MEDITATION MOJO

Get into a meditative high and position and contemplate the following: What makes you feel safe? What makes you feel secure? What makes you feel loved? How do you create these feelings for yourself? If you wish, journal after your meditation.

JUNE 26
HERBAL BLENDS

Create this blend for inner peace.

You will need:

- Hops (dried)
- Lavender (dried)
- Catnip (dried)
- Blue vervain (dried)
- Lemon balm (dried)
- Tulsi (dried)
- Rose (dried)
- Chamomile (dried)

Combine equal amounts of the herbs, then grind them together and combine with weed in a one-to-one ratio. Use it whenever you need to relieve anxiety, anger, sadness, or other negative emotions. This blend can be smoked or used as tea.

Use this blend on its own for a boost or to accompany your peace-themed spellwork. Focus on the peace you are seeking as you combine and grind your herbs together, infusing the blend with your intention and energy.

Add this recipe, how it feels, and your results to your Book of Shadows. If you desire, adjust ratios for flavor.

JUNE 27
FIND YOUR WILD

Connect to the night sky with a good high. You do not have to see the stars with your physical eyes if you picture them in your mind's eye. A galaxy map can show you where you are in relation to constellations and the moon to help you get your bearings and give you images to visualize.

Stand outside in the dark with your face to the sky. Either stare into space, taking in everything you can see—the stars, the moon, even satellites and airplanes cutting across the sky—or if it is too cloudy or your view is disrupted by light pollution, picture them in your mind. The energies of air and celestial bodies are all around you. How do these energies feel to you? How do you differentiate them from one another? How can you best utilize them? Add this information to your BOS.

This exercise will be done monthly throughout the year because as the night sky changes, the energies you feel will also change.

JUNE 28
MAGICAL MUSICAL MOVEMENT

Start a playlist of songs that make you feel peaceful. This playlist can be used when you want to add to your prepping and spellwork or create a peaceful setting for meditation or other workings.

Try out your playlist by getting high and choosing a few songs to move to in whatever type of movement you prefer, even if it is only rocking back and forth. Move to the music in a way that helps create and support your sense of peace.

Try listening to your playlist motionless with your eyes closed or with a blindfold to block out other distractions. Use headphones if possible. Does it create the peaceful energy and emotion you desired?

JUNE 29
INTRIGUING INCANTATIONS

When life feels chaotic and you need to release tension, use this chant to sing in harmony.

> *Stress and anxiety, I demand to cease.*
> *Bottled up negativity, I do release.*

Positive vibes I call to increase,
Fill my heart and soul with peace.

Use this chant on its own or with other spellwork.

JUNE 30
SOULFUL SEARCHING

Reflect on the previous month. In what ways were you able to bring peace into your life? How can you make your life even more peaceful? Meditate and journal on your overall experiences and how they contributed to your practice, spirituality, or both.

July

With summer at its height, the natural energies in the universe are strong, bold, and full of life. It is an ideal time to tap into these energies to develop and intensify your abilities in working with them. This month, work on increasing your psychic skills while focusing on tapping into these energies.

July Supply List
July 2

> 5 × 5-inch square piece of black material
>
> Jet (small stone or chips)

Lapis lazuli (small stone or chips)

Essential oil, dried herb, or resin: cedar, juniper, dragon's blood, catnip, sage, thyme, clove, frankincense

Dried: mugwort, High John the Conqueror root, wormwood

6 inches of silver ribbon or thread

Cannabis incense (optional for nonsmokers)

July 8

Your water charger

Mugwort

Sage

Sweet woodruff

Wormwood

Amethyst

Moonstone

Obsidian

July 14

Cannabis incense (optional for nonsmokers)

July 15

Carnelian

July 16

White sage

July 17

Fresh-picked dandelion heads

Frankincense resin

Fresh or dried: blue vervain, lavender buds, mugwort, sacred lotus petals, wormwood, cannabis

July 18

Candle

Lighter

July 19

Lavender

July 20

Your water charger

Catnip

Cinnamon

Clove

Mugwort

Wormwood

Amethyst

Obsidian

July 21

Lemon peel

Rubbing alcohol

Table salt

July 24

Black candle

Lighter

Cannabis incense (optional for nonsmokers)

July 26

Blue vervain

Calea zacatechichi

Catnip

Mugwort

Mullein

Peppermint

Rose

Wormwood

July 30

Jar with removable lid or corked vial

Fresh, dried, or essential oil: dragon's blood, eucalyptus, peppermint, feverfew, ginger

Lemon peel (dried)

Garlic cloves

Cannabis (dried)

JULY 1
LIT LITERATURE

Psychic development is an important topic, as not only does it help you learn to access and use different skills, but it also teaches you what the different skills of psychic development are. Even if you find yourself having little to no success when you first begin psychic development exercises, you are learning what the skills are, how to use them, and what types of exercises help you grow in proficiency. Having the knowledge and understanding of how to use the tools does not guarantee skill level, but it does give you the foundation to build your practice on. Skill comes with focused practice. It also lets you know where your interests lie and where they don't.

No matter where you shop for books, use the keywords "psychic development" or "ESP" (extrasensory perception) in your search to find titles of interest.

JULY 2
TEMPTING TALISMAN

Create this talisman to aid you in your psychic work. Try to use a mix of oils and dried ingredients if available to you. Use a pinch of dried ingredients and a drop or two of oils.

You will need:

- 5 × 5-inch square piece of black material
- Jet (small stone or chips)
- Lapis lazuli (small stone or chips)
- Cedar (essential oil, dried herb, or resin)
- Juniper (essential oil, dried herb, or resin)
- Dragon's blood (essential oil, dried herb, or resin)
- Catnip (essential oil, dried herb, or resin)
- Sage (essential oil, dried herb, or resin)
- Thyme (essential oil, dried herb, or resin)

- Clove (essential oil, dried herb, or resin)
- Frankincense (essential oil, dried herb, or resin)
- Mugwort (dried)
- High John the Conqueror root (dried)
- Wormwood (dried)
- 6 inches of silver ribbon or thread
- Cannabis incense (optional for nonsmokers)

Smoke your weed (or use another consumption method) while you assemble your ingredients and create this talisman. If you have room to work at your altar, do so, or create another sacred space where you have room and are comfortable.

Lay the black square on your altar or other stable location. Begin with the largest ingredients you are working with, most likely your stones in this instance. Add them to the center of the material.

Next, add any smaller dried herbs or flowers. Top these off with one drop of any essential oils you use. Drip them onto a dried herb or flower so they soak into those instead of the material.

When you are done filling it, bunch the material up into a pouch and wrap the ribbon around the neck three times before knotting it off.

Use this chant to help guide your intentions and work:

Charge this talisman to help my sight,
With clean and clear visions right.
Infuse it with our magic combined,
Energies together, theirs and mine.

Take a hit and release your intention and exhale your smoke all over the pouch. (You may also use the smoke from cannabis incense along with your own breath.)

Store your talisman on your altar or in another magical, safe space. Hold it to your heart and then your third eye, accompanied by deep breathing, when you need to use its stored energy. Keep it near you when working a divination session to increase your psychic awareness and skills.

JULY 3
SOULFUL SEARCHING

Get high and meditate on your past relationships. What aspects were successful? What aspects were not? What have you learned from failed ones? What have you learned from successful ones?

JULY 4
ASTROLOGICAL HOUSES

Research the meaning of the astrological seventh house and explore the role it plays in your life within your own chart. The seventh house represents your relationships. Record the information you learn and how it relates to your sign and yourself in your Book of Shadows or a journal.

JULY 5
EMBRACING THE ELEMENTS

Collect a jar of dirt for your witch's cupboard. Backyard dirt is used in workings dealing with the family, home, and property, including protection and drawing in peace. When you can, you should collect the dirt from each corner of the property at the boundaries. If you live in an apartment or other situation in which there is no dirt around, the dirt from a houseplant also works.

JULY 6
CERRIDWEN'S CAULDRON

Evaluate your current level of psychic abilities. Which abilities do you feel you possess? What is your proficiency level? What psychic skills would you like to develop or enhance? Add your psychic resume to your Book of Shadows and take steps to research aspects you want to learn or improve.

JULY 7
LIFTED PERSPECTIVE

Consume your cannabis and connect with your higher self in a meditative state. Step back and look at yourself objectively; allow your walls to slip away.

Which perspective do you operate from: Are you a giver? A taker? Or a matcher? What do you give to others? What do you take from others? What types of relationship transactions do you make? Journal about your meditation.

JULY 8
DELIGHTFUL DABBLING

Using your water charger, combine water and earth together in this bong water herbal infusion for divination.

You will need:

- Your water charger
- Mugwort
- Sage
- Sweet woodruff
- Wormwood
- Amethyst
- Moonstone
- Obsidian

You may either add the mugwort, sage, sweet woodruff, and wormwood to the water to steep or place the plant matter with the amethyst, moonstone, and obsidian separate from your water but in close proximity. Use this water in your bong (or drink) to open yourself psychically to perform a divination session.

JULY 9
FIND YOUR WILD

Find a place to take a nature break today and seek out the natural energies of summer. After you get high, spend at least fifteen minutes outside, preferably in a location with as few other people and distractions as possible. Close your eyes and tune out all human-caused energies around you. Eliminate manufactured sounds and scents. Allow yourself several minutes to adjust to the energies around you and shuffle through them, marking those you can for ignoring. What natural forces can you detect? What do you hear? What do you smell? What do you feel in the air?

JULY 10
EMBRACING THE ELEMENTS

While moon water is more commonly used, sun water also exists and combines the energies of water with the fiery power of the sun. In July, the sun is at its strongest for those in the Northern Hemisphere—the perfect time to make sun water to harness the bright, warm, joyous energies of the sun, which are often lacking in availability during the winter.

Use a glass container to charge water under the rays of the sun, and then pour it into airtight jars or freeze for use in the winter. When you need a boost from the sun's energy in the winter, add some of the water to your bong or bathwater, or use it however else it is needed.

JULY 11
GROWING WITH THE GREEN MAN

Choose an outdoor location where it's safe for you to be high and sit for a while. Take notice of all forms of life around you, whether it's plants, animals, or even other people.

Close your eyes and use your different senses. What do you hear? What do you smell? What life forms can you feel? Detect and distinguish the energies around you.

JULY 12
SUPERNATURAL SENSES

Astral travel is an out-of-body experience that may be achieved either while awake or asleep in which the practitioner projects their consciousness to somewhere else on the earthly plane. It may feel like soaring as you arrive at your chosen destination.

A deep meditative high will help to cut the strings and allow the practitioner's mind to take off and fly to familiar lands or places unknown.

Choose a familiar location to visit. Get high and lie down in a comfortable position with your eyes closed. Focus on the location you want to visit and allow your high to carry you there. Cut any strings you feel holding you down. Go to your location and observe everything you can.

Document your experiences in your BOS and be sure to update it as new events occur.

JULY 13
RECLAIMING THE SHADOW

Ditch weed is fake. It's not the real thing. It won't give you the results you want.

Get into a deep meditative high and connect with your higher self or power. Answer the questions, How have you been untrue to yourself? How have you been untrue to others? Listen for and accept the answers you receive and document them in your journal.

JULY 14
DANK DIVINATION

Smoke or vape your weed and blow the smoke over your tarot or oracle cards as you shuffle them, focusing on a relationship you wish to explore in your reading. (You may also consume your cannabis in a different manner and use the smoke from cannabis incense.) Lay out eight cards in a line to read as follows:

Card 1. Your current self.

Card 2. The role you believe you play in the relationship.

Card 3. The role you actively play in the relationship.

Card 4. Strengths of the relationship.

Card 5. Weaknesses of the relationship.

Card 6. Your strengths in the relationship.

Card 7. Your weaknesses in the relationship.

Card 8. How the relationship can grow.

Document your drawn cards and their meanings in your journal. Explore your reading in meditation.

JULY 15
DELIGHTFUL DABBLING

Charge your weed with carnelian to infuse it with energies for creativity, energy, fire work, and connection with the divine masculine.

For a quick infusion, hold your weed (or other cannabis product) in your nondominant hand with your carnelian in your dominant hand. Move the carnelian all over and around the weed and say:

Send your energies from here to there,
Infuse this [weed, gummy, THC, etc.]
With fiery energy to nourish
My spirit with blessed creativity.

For a deeper charge, dedicate a small box, chest, or other type of container where you can charge your cannabis by placing it, along with a carnelian stone, inside.

JULY 16
SACRED SMOKE

While white sage is known for its purification and cleansing qualities, when consumed it helps induce a meditative state and connect you with your higher self. White sage helps relieve feelings of being overwhelmed and promotes self-awareness. Be sure to obtain yours from an ethical source or grow your own since it's an endangered plant and sacred to Indigenous people.

Introduce yourself to white sage by using it on its own several times first, exploring it with all your senses. How does it look? Smell? Feel? Taste? You may either smoke it or make a tealike infusion by soaking the leaves in hot water to drink.

How does it affect you? What do you feel when using it? How long does it take to feel the effects? How long do the effects last?

Evaluate and learn how white sage works with your body and mind. Document this information in your Book of Shadows. Once you become familiar with this herb, combine it with cannabis and again explore the effects, being sure to document your results.

JULY 17
KITCHEN WITCHERY

In the morning, combine the following ingredients in a pot of water to simmer throughout the day. Use this on days when you want to increase your psychic awareness for divination purposes. Be sure to start your simmer pot at least a couple of hours before your divination workings so it has time to simmer and get the energies and magic started around you.

You will need:

- Handful of fresh-picked dandelion heads
- 1 teaspoon frankincense resin
- 1 teaspoon blue vervain (fresh or dried)
- 1 teaspoon lavender buds (fresh or dried)
- 1 tablespoon mugwort (fresh or dried)
- 1 tablespoon sacred lotus petals (fresh or dried)
- 1 teaspoon wormwood (fresh or dried)
- Pinch of cannabis (fresh or dried)

As you prepare the ingredients and add them to the pot, pour intention into your work.

Keep the pot on a low flame on a back burner. Stir the pot nine times clockwise once every hour throughout the day.

Each time you stir the pot, say:

Fire, water, earth, and air,
My magic has a little flare.
Fruits from the earth simmer here.
Increase my skills, draw [energy or energies, spirits,
    or guardians] near.

Add more water as needed to replenish what has evaporated. At the end of the day, pour the remains outside on the ground near a tree or under a bush. Return the plant material to the earth it came from. Add this recipe to your BOS and record your own experience with it.

JULY 18
DELIGHTFUL DABBLING

Use a candle in a color that corresponds to your working to light joints or a hemp wick, which will then be used to light other things such as pipes and bongs.

You will need:

- Candle
- Lighter

Candle color correspondences

Black: banishing, binding, boundaries, challenges, crossroads, darkness, death, divination, endings, hexing, the otherworld or underworld, protection, psychic abilities

Blue: astral realm, calming, clarity, dream work, hope, inspiration, intuition, optimism, purification, spirituality, truth, visions

Brown: concentration, decision-making, family, grounding, justice, longevity, loss, stability, success

Gold: abundance, confidence, consecration, creativity, divination, divine masculine, energy, healing, intuition, knowledge, money, power, security, strength, success, wisdom

Green: abundance, acceptance, accomplishment, balance, business, change, energy, fertility, good health, growth, healing, life, luck, money, nature spirits, prosperity, rebirth, renewal, success, wealth

Orange: action, ambition, change, confidence, courage, creativity, energy, matters of the mind, passion, stimulation, support

Pink: affection, calming, compassion, friendship, harmony, love, nurturing, peace, romance, sensual, stress relieving

Purple: divination, enlightenment, freedom, inspiration, intuition, protection, psychic abilities, spirit contact, spirituality, truth, visions

Red: action, ambition, anger, courage, creativity, danger, desire, destruction, emotions, energy, life, longevity, love, passion, power, sex, willpower

Silver: astral realm, clairvoyance, divination, divine feminine, dream work, inspiration, intuition,

moon magic, power, protection, psychic abilities,
spirituality, success

White: astral realm, balance, blessings, concentration, death, divination, gratitude, harmony, hope,
innocence, light, protection, purification, self-
work, spirituality, truth

Yellow: action, cheerfulness, clarity, communication,
community, creativity, focus, happiness, imagination, intelligence, light, stimulation, warmth,
wisdom

Choose a color that represents what you want to draw
into your life. Light your candle, consume your THC (lighting it with your candle if you smoke), and stare into the
flame for several minutes, focusing on what it is you seek.

JULY 19
ETHEREAL ESSENCES

Research the different correspondences and uses associated
with lavender and add a supply to your witch's cupboard. Add
the information you find to your BOS. Dried lavender can be
smoked, combined with cannabis, or made into a tea. Meet the
essence of lavender in the following meditative practice.

Get into an elevated high and comfortable position with a small container of dried lavender, a bottle of oil, or incense lit and placed in front of you.

Close your eyes and take several deep breaths. Allow your mind to settle and focus. When you are ready, pick up the lavender and hold it about four inches away from your nose. Inhale the scent, breathing deeply. If it's not too overpowering for you, move it closer. Some people have sensitivities, so don't feel you have to move it directly under your nose. Oils are very potent and do not need to be moved as close.

How does this scent make you feel? Is it pleasing? Irritating? Relaxing? Exciting? Powerful? Meditate on the feelings it evokes in you.

Journal about your experience. If you feel the need to clear the scent from your nose, sniff coffee beans or grounds to help neutralize the scent.

JULY 20
HERBAL INFUSIONS

Using your water charger, combine water and earth together in this bong water herbal infusion to boost your psychic awareness.

You will need:

- Your water charger
- Catnip

- Cinnamon
- Clove
- Mugwort
- Wormwood
- Amethyst
- Obsidian

You may either add the herbs to the water to steep or place the plant matter with the amethyst and obsidian separate from your water but in close proximity. Use this water in your bong (or drink) to enhance your skills.

JULY 21
VIBING

Clean your cannabis equipment with a zesty, positive vibe.

You will need:

- Lemon peel
- Rubbing alcohol
- Table salt

Soak the lemon peel in rubbing alcohol (the longer the better) and use it along with table salt (give it a quick blessing) to scrub away negativity and residue for a new, shiny, positive outlook.

JULY 22
SOULFUL SEARCHING

Connect to your higher self in a deeply meditative, trancelike high. Ask your higher self (or power) to show you a past life. What do you see? Who are you? Where are you from? When are you from? Why was this incarnation the one chosen to be shown? What message or reminder does Spirit have for you? Journal about your experience.

JULY 23
RECLAIMING THE SHADOW

Get into a deep meditative high and connect with your higher self or power.

Answer the questions, Where do I waste my energy? Why do I do this? What could I do instead? How can I redirect myself to reclaim my energy? Journal about your answers and set goals for changing your patterns.

JULY 24
DANK DIVINATION

Use this divination session to interpret messages through a candle flame.

You will need:

- Black candle
- Lighter
- Cannabis incense (optional for nonsmokers)

In a dark or dimly lit room, light a black candle and place it in front of you.

Smoke or vape your weed, and as you exhale, gently blow the smoke around the flame without blowing it out. Focus on opening your mind to receiving images through the flame. (You may also consume your cannabis in a different manner and use the smoke from cannabis incense.)

Record your experience in your Book of Shadows along with any information you obtain through research on pyromancy.

JULY 25
MEDITATION MOJO

Get into a meditative high and position to contemplate what values you hold close to your heart. What truths do you hold to be self-evident? How do these values affect your spirituality? Journal after your meditation.

JULY 26
HERBAL BLENDS

Create this blend for divination.

You will need:

- Blue vervain
- *Calea zacatechichi*
- Catnip
- Mugwort
- Mullein
- Peppermint
- Rose
- Wormwood

Start by combining equal amounts of the herbs. Grind them together and then combine with weed in a one-to-one ratio. Use before and during your work as you like. This blend can be smoked or used as tea.

Use this blend on its own for a boost or to accompany your divination work. Focus on the energies you are seeking as you combine and grind your herbs together, infusing the blend with your intention and energy.

Add this recipe, how it feels, and your results to your Book of Shadows. If you desire, adjust ratios for flavor.

JULY 27
FIND YOUR WILD

Connect to the night sky with a good high. You do not have to see the stars with your physical eyes if you picture them in your mind's eye. A galaxy map can show you where you are in relation to constellations and the moon to help you get your bearings and give you images to visualize.

Stand outside in the dark with your face to the sky. Either stare into space, taking in everything you can see—the stars, the moon, even satellites and airplanes cutting across the sky—or if it is too cloudy or your view is disrupted by light pollution, picture them in your mind. The energies of air and celestial bodies are all around you. How do these energies feel to you? How do you differentiate them from one another? How can you best utilize them? Add this information to your BOS.

This exercise will be done monthly throughout the year because as the night sky changes, the energies you feel will also change.

JULY 28
MAGICAL MUSICAL MOVEMENT

Start a playlist of songs that help you focus during psychic workings. This playlist can be used when you want to add to your prepping and spellwork, to raise energy, or when you are in a divination session or other type of working. Check out several types of frequency-based music to see how they work for you.

Try out your playlist by getting high and choosing a few songs to move to in whatever type of movement you prefer, even if it is only rocking back and forth. Move to the music to connect with its energy.

Try listening to your playlist motionless with your eyes closed or with a blindfold to block out other distractions. Use headphones if possible. Does it create the environment and energy you desired?

JULY 29
INTRIGUING INCANTATIONS

Ritual helps us switch from the mundane world to the spiritual world. When preparing for divination or other psychic workings, using a chant gives your mind the cue it is time to change modes.

Use this chant to invite in your higher self, a deity or deities, or other spirit guides. Say:

> *Be my guide in this need,*
> *Send me signs that I can read.*
> *Open my mind to see and hear,*
> *What my eyes and ears can deny is there.*
> *Help me to see with my inner sight,*
> *Watch over my working, bless this rite.*

Add this chant to your Book of Shadows.

JULY 30
DELIGHTFUL DABBLING

Create this spell jar to heal your physical self. It's a perfect remedy for a summer cold. You won't be permanently sealing this jar, but you will want an easy-open lid with a good seal to help keep the ingredients fresh and accessible for you to inhale several times a day.

You will need:

- Jar with removable lid or corked vial
- Dragon's blood (fresh, dried, or essential oil)
- Eucalyptus (fresh, dried, or essential oil)
- Peppermint (fresh, dried, or essential oil)
- Feverfew (fresh, dried, or essential oil)
- Ginger (fresh, dried, or essential oil)
- Lemon peel (dried)
- Garlic cloves
- Cannabis (dried)

Smoke your weed (or use another consumption method, allowing time for edibles to take effect).

Layer each ingredient into your chosen jar, focusing on each one's energy along with your intention.

As you work with each ingredient, say:

> I call upon the energies of [ingredient name],
> Heal me!

Take a hit (or deep, centered, intention-filled breath if you do not smoke or vape) and use your exhalation to gently blow your hopes and objectives into your jar.

Close the top of the jar. When finished, say:

Combine together,
To make me strong,
Heal my body,
Right what is wrong.

Store in the refrigerator. Every few hours, take a deep inhalation of the scent, filling your lungs with its antibacterial and healing properties. When you feel better, empty the jar and safely burn the ingredients.

JULY 31
SOULFUL SEARCHING

Think back over how you worked with the energies of the natural world this past month, especially as a source of power for your psychic practices. Meditate and journal on your overall experiences and how they contributed to your practice, spirituality, or both.

August

This month, enjoy the magic of creativity. How do you currently use creativity in your practice? Try innovative ideas and explore new creative possibilities.

August Supply List

August 2

6 × 6-inch square piece of orange material

Moonstone (piece or chips)

Birch bark (dried)

Essential oil, dried herb, or resin: carnation, lilac, vervain, patchouli

6 inches of red ribbon

Cannabis incense (optional for nonsmokers)

August 5

Glass jar with lid or corked vial

Dragon's blood resin

Dried: basil, garlic, thyme, coriander, cumin, motherwort

Salt

Cannabis

Blue sealing wax

Yellow sealing wax

Brown sealing wax

August 8

Your water charger

Chamomile

Dill

Clear quartz

Green aventurine

August 14

Cannabis incense (optional for nonsmokers)

August 16

Skullcap

August 17

Apple thinly sliced into rounds

Fresh mushrooms (oyster is preferable)

Fresh or dried: chamomile buds, daisy petals, orris
    root, skullcap, cannabis

August 18

Citrine

August 19

Coriander

August 20

Apple juice

Cherry juice

Pomegranate juice (grenadine)

Maple syrup

Chamomile (dried)

Cloves

Cinnamon

August 22

Glass jar with lid or corked vial

Dragon's blood (resin)

Dried: mugwort, mullein, wormwood, wild lettuce, *Calea zacatechichi*, sacred lotus petals, blue lotus petals, blue vervain, white sage

Cannabis ash

Black sealing wax

Purple sealing wax

August 24

> Your water charger
>
> Mugwort
>
> Wormwood
>
> Lavender
>
> Amethyst
>
> Moonstone

August 26

> Dried: mugwort, wormwood, sakae naa leaf, peppermint, blue vervain

August 30

> Glass jar with lid or corked vial
>
> Cloves
>
> Frankincense
>
> Mistletoe
>
> Myrrh
>
> Nettle
>
> Black peppercorns
>
> Crushed red pepper
>
> Thistle

Hyssop

Cannabis ash

Small piece of paper

Writing instrument

Black sealing wax

Enough black twine to wrap around the top of
your jar and tie on a charm

"X" charm

Cannabis incense (optional for nonsmokers)

AUGUST 1
LIT LITERATURE

Even if you never grow your own cannabis, learning about the growing and harvesting process is not only educational, but it also helps build an understanding and closer connection to the final product you use.

No matter where you shop for books, use the keywords "cannabis cultivation" or "books on growing cannabis" in your search to find titles of interest.

AUGUST 2
TEMPTING TALISMAN

Boost your creativity with this energetic talisman. Try to use a mix of oils and dried ingredients if available to you. Use a pinch of dried ingredients and a drop or two of oils.

You will need:

- 6 × 6-inch square piece of orange material
- Moonstone (piece or chips)
- Birch bark (dried)
- Carnation (essential oil, dried herb, or resin)
- Lilac (essential oil, dried herb, or resin)
- Vervain (essential oil, dried herb, or resin)
- Patchouli (essential oil, dried herb, or resin)
- 6 inches of red ribbon
- Cannabis incense (optional for nonsmokers)

Smoke your weed (or use another consumption method) while you assemble your ingredients and create this talisman. If you have room to work at your altar, do so, or create another sacred space where you have room and are comfortable.

Lay the orange square on your altar or other stable location. Begin with the largest ingredients you are working with, most likely your moonstone in this instance. Add them to the center of the material.

Next, add any smaller dried herbs, resins, or chips. Top these off with one drop of any essential oils you use. Drip them onto a dried herb, bark, or flower so they soak into those instead of the material.

When you are done filling it, bunch the material up into a pouch and wrap the ribbon around the neck three times before knotting it off. Trim off any extra material if you like.

Use this chant to help guide your intentions and work:

When a muse is what I need,
Send inspiration here to me.
Fill my imagination
With bright possibilities,
Bring visions to mind,
Energize my abilities.

Take a hit and release your intention and exhale your smoke all over the pouch. (You may also use the smoke from cannabis incense along with your own breath.)

You may place your talisman under your pillow to help draw creative energies to you while you sleep. Place it on your desk or other work area, or carry it on your person if you need a boost of creativity.

AUGUST 3
SOULFUL SEARCHING

Get high and meditate on the ways you express creativity and how you express yourself creatively. Creativity and talent are not the same thing. You do not have to excel at a certain type of creativity to enjoy participating in it. What forms of creativity do you enjoy? Which do you find difficult to partake in? Which forms inspire you? Journal about your experience.

AUGUST 4
ASTROLOGICAL HOUSES

Research the meaning of the astrological eighth house and explore the role it plays in your life within your own chart. The eighth house represents death and rebirth. Record the information you learn and how it relates to your sign and yourself in your Book of Shadows or a journal.

AUGUST 5
DELIGHTFUL DABBLING

This spell jar is to ensure and keep a cheerful home. If you live with other people and can get them to create this spell jar with you, all the better. You can take turns adding ingredients to combine all your energies together.

You will need:

- Glass jar with lid or corked vial
- Dragon's blood resin
- Basil (dried)
- Garlic (dried)
- Thyme (dried)
- Coriander (dried)
- Cumin (dried)
- Motherwort (dried)
- Salt
- Cannabis
- Blue sealing wax
- Yellow sealing wax
- Brown sealing wax

Smoke your weed (or use another consumption method, allowing time for edibles to take effect).

Place each ingredient into your chosen jar (or mix them in a bowl and then transfer them to your jar), focusing on each one's energy along with your intention of creating and maintaining a content home.

As you work with each ingredient, say:

> *I call upon the energies of [ingredient name],*
> *Bless this home with peace and happiness.*

Take a hit (or deep, centered, intention-filled breath if you do not smoke or vape) and use your exhalation to gently blow your hopes and objectives into your jar.

Close the top of the jar and cover it in the melted sealing wax, first blue, then add the brown and yellow on top so that some of each color is visible.

When finished, say:

> *Within these walls,*
> *The space [I or we] call home,*
> *Protect [me or us] here,*
> *Keep [me or us] safe and sound.*
> *Create an aura of calm,*
> *Positivity, and peace.*
> *With this spell,*
> *[My or our] happiness increased.*

Display the jar in a prominent location in your home. A family room is ideal.

AUGUST 6
CERRIDWEN'S CAULDRON

What types of creativity and artistic expression do you currently partake in? How do you currently incorporate these into your Craft or spiritual practice?

Explore a new form of creativity or artistic expression. How can you incorporate this into your practice? What new skills does it teach you?

AUGUST 7
LIFTED PERSPECTIVE

Treat yourself today with a happy break. Let yourself get as high as you like and allow any worries to disappear for a little while.

Conjure up a vision of something fun and exciting you would like to do—anything you can imagine. There are no limits. Let your mind, and your high, take you on your adventure. Where did you go and what did you do?

AUGUST 8
DELIGHTFUL DABBLING

Using your water charger, combine water and earth together in this bong water herbal infusion.

You will need:

- Your water charger
- Chamomile
- Dill
- Clear quartz
- Green aventurine

You may either add the chamomile and dill to the water to steep or place the plant matter with the quartz and aventurine separate from your water but in close proximity. Use this water in your bong (or drink) to help draw prosperity to your life.

AUGUST 9
FIND YOUR WILD

Explore aquatic life and the energies of distinct species that resonate with you. This may require advanced planning, so, if necessary, use today for research on where you can find aquatic life to observe. If local or native aquatic life is inaccessible, don't rule out aquariums, pet or gardening shops, or pond supply stores. While these may not be the most ideal situations, they are options that exist. (The energies you encounter may be altered by the environment in which they are contained.)

Observe your chosen aquatic life. What lessons does it have for you? What vibes do you receive?

AUGUST 10
EMBRACING THE ELEMENTS

The element of air is a channel or transportation system in which other types of energy travel throughout your surroundings. Innumerable energies exist all around you, carried around on the breeze, floating through the atmosphere. What energies can you pluck from your environment to utilize in your magical practice?

AUGUST 11
GROWING WITH THE GREEN MAN

Get high and experience the different energies of sunlight and shadow. Find an area outside where you can sit in both the sun and the shade. Sit for a while in the sun, a while longer in the shade, and then try to sit or lie down with part of your body in the sunshine and part in the shade.

Pay attention to the differences in the energies you detect and how you feel enveloped in them. Journal about what you feel and your observations.

AUGUST 12
SUPERNATURAL SENSES

Sense the sunrise. Verify what time sunrise will be this morning (or tomorrow if necessary) for this exercise. Experience as much of the sunrise as possible, even if it means only sensing it from your own bed. What shifts in energy can you feel with the rising of the sun?

AUGUST 13
RECLAIMING THE SHADOW

Chronic is the best of the best. Begin this exercise by journaling about your best traits. When you run out of ideas, get high and try again from your higher self. If you are able to add to your list, what traits did you miss?

AUGUST 14
DANK DIVINATION

Smoke or vape your weed and blow the smoke over your tarot or oracle cards as you shuffle them, focusing on connecting to Spirit for this objective reading of yourself in relation to service and sacrifice. (You may consume your cannabis in a different form and use the smoke from cannabis incense.) Lay out eight cards in a line for this reading.

Card 1. My beliefs on service.

Card 2. Where I excel in service.

Card 3. My weaknesses related to service.

Card 4. My beliefs on sacrifice.

Card 5. Where I excel in regard to sacrifice.

Card 6. What are my weaknesses in regard to sacrifice?

Card 7. What do I need to learn in regard to service?

Card 8. What do I need to learn in regard to sacrifice?

Document your drawn cards and their meanings in your journal. Explore your reading in meditation.

AUGUST 15
SOULFUL SEARCHING

This month's astrological house deals with death and rebirth. Meditate and then journal about how these themes have influenced you. What did you experience and how did these events shape your life? How do these themes play a role in your spiritual practice?

AUGUST 16
SACRED SMOKE

Skullcap both soothes the mind and increases mental focus to aid in a meditative state.

Introduce yourself to skullcap by using it on its own several times first, exploring it with all your senses. How does it look? Smell? Feel? Taste? You may either smoke it or make a tealike infusion by soaking the leaves in hot water to drink.

How does it affect you? What do you feel when using it? How long does it take to feel the effects? How long do the effects last?

Evaluate and learn how skullcap works with your body and mind. Document this information in your Book of Shadows. Once you become familiar with this herb, combine it with cannabis and again explore the effects, being sure to document your results.

AUGUST 17
KITCHEN WITCHERY

In the morning, combine the following ingredients in a pot of water to simmer throughout the day. Use this on days when you want to boost your creativity. Be sure to start your simmer pot early so it has time to simmer and get the energies and magic started around you.

You will need:

- 1 apple thinly sliced into rounds
- 3 fresh mushrooms (oyster is preferable)
- 1 teaspoon chamomile buds (fresh or dried)
- 1 teaspoon daisy petals (fresh or dried)
- 1 teaspoon orris root (fresh or dried)
- 1 teaspoon skullcap (fresh or dried)
- Pinch of cannabis (fresh or dried)

As you prepare the ingredients and add them to the pot, pour intention into your work.

Keep the pot on a low flame on a back burner. Stir the pot nine times clockwise once every hour throughout the day.

Each time you stir the pot, say:

Fire, water, earth, and air,
My magic has a little flare.
Fruits from the earth simmer here.
A creative boost, I summon—appear!

Add more water as needed to replenish what has evaporated. At the end of the day, pour the remains outside on the ground near a tree or under a bush. Return the plant material to the earth it came from. Add this recipe to your BOS and record your own experience with it.

AUGUST 18
DELIGHTFUL DABBLING

Charge your weed with citrine to infuse it with energies for confidence, joy, and learning.

For a quick infusion, hold your weed (or other cannabis product) in your nondominant hand with your citrine in your dominant hand. Move the citrine all over and around the weed and say:

Send your energies from here to there,
Infuse this [weed, gummy, THC, etc.]
With citrine's care.

Store the power for magic's sake,
For me to use when I get baked.

For a deeper charge, dedicate a small box, chest, or other type of container where you can charge your cannabis by placing it, along with a citrine stone or chips, inside.

AUGUST 19
ETHEREAL ESSENCES

Research the different correspondences and uses associated with coriander and add a supply to your witch's cupboard. Add the information you find to your BOS. Dried coriander can be smoked, combined with cannabis, or made into a tea. Meet the essence of coriander in the following meditative practice.

Get into an elevated high and comfortable position with a small container of dried coriander, a bottle of oil, or incense lit and placed in front of you.

Close your eyes and take several deep breaths. Allow your mind to settle and focus. When you are ready, pick up the coriander and hold it about four inches away from your nose. Inhale the scent, breathing deeply. If it's not too overpowering for you, move it closer. Some people have sensitivities, so don't feel you have to move it directly under your nose. Oils are very potent and do not need to be moved as close.

How does this scent make you feel? Is it pleasing? Irritating? Relaxing? Exciting? Powerful? Meditate on the feelings it evokes in you.

Journal about your experience. If you feel the need to clear the scent from your nose, sniff coffee beans or grounds to help neutralize the scent.

AUGUST 20
HERBAL INFUSIONS

Combine water and earth together in this herbal infusion beverage for creativity.

You will need:

- 8 ounces apple juice
- 1 ounce cherry juice
- 1 ounce pomegranate juice (grenadine)
- 2 teaspoons maple syrup
- 2 teaspoons chamomile
- 3 cloves
- Cinnamon

Either in a microwave or on a stovetop, gently warm the three juices together to a light simmer. Stir in the maple syrup. Add the chamomile and cloves to a tea bag or strainer. Pour the juice blend into a mug and add the tea bag or strainer. Allow to steep for five minutes, remove bag or strainer, and top off with a light sprinkling of cinnamon. Sip this warm drink and let inspiration flow.

AUGUST 21
VIBING

Everything vibrates. The number of cycles a vibration completes in one second is the frequency. Extremely high (ultrasonic) or low (infrasound) frequencies can cause damage to the human body. The ideal frequency for optimal cognitive functioning is 40 Hz.

Use a search engine or music service to find 40-Hz music to listen to, preferably with headphones. Get high to experience how this frequency feels to you, then journal about your experience.

AUGUST 22
DELIGHTFUL DABBLING

Create this spell jar to boost your abilities when using your psychic insight.

You will need:

- Glass jar with lid or corked vial
- Dragon's blood (resin)
- Mugwort (dried)
- Mullein (dried)
- Wormwood (dried)
- Wild lettuce (dried)
- *Calea zacatechichi* (dried)
- Sacred lotus petals (dried)
- Blue lotus petals (dried)
- Blue vervain (dried)
- White sage (dried)
- Cannabis ash
- Black sealing wax
- Purple sealing wax

Smoke your weed (or use another consumption method, allowing time for edibles to take effect).

Place each ingredient into your chosen jar (or mix them in a bowl and then transfer them to your jar), focusing on each one's energy along with your intention.

As you work with each ingredient, say:

I call upon the energies of [ingredient name],
Your power is needed,
I call it to me.

Take a hit (or deep, centered, intention-filled breath if you do not smoke or vape) and use your exhalation to gently blow your hopes and objectives into your jar.

Close the top of the jar and cover it with the melted black sealing wax and then the purple wax, allowing some of the black wax to still be seen. When finished, say:

In this vessel is magic contained,
To amplify my power with energy tamed.
Find the visions, I need to see,
Send them here, send them to me.

Store this jar on your altar or in another safe magical location. When you need it, hold it to your third eye and repeat the chant above. Place it close to you or on your person when you need the boost of energy for psychic insight.

AUGUST 23
RECLAIMING THE SHADOW

Making the unconscious a part of our everyday consciousness is how we begin to heal. This is the basis of shadow work. When we heal, we become more whole, allowing for greater connections with natural energies with fewer blockages and distractions to get in the way. These connections in turn lead us to more healing—a preferred cycle to the ones we often live. Meditate on this healing process. What message does your subconscious want to become conscious of today? Document your results in your journal.

AUGUST 24
DANK DIVINATION

Bong users will enjoy this fun divination exercise as you scrutinize your bong smoke for images or visions. In order to have enough smoke for this exercise, you'll need to be smoking. If you're a nonsmoker, skip this day and use one of the extra days provided in other chapters.

You will need:

- Your water charger
- Mugwort

- Wormwood

- Lavender

- Amethyst

- Moonstone

Create your bong water mix by either adding the mugwort, wormwood, and lavender to the water to steep or placing the herbs with the amethyst and moonstone separate from your water but in close proximity. A clear round bong (one of the fortune-teller crystal ball designs is really cool for this practice!) is perfect for this divination method if available.

Next, combine equal parts mugwort, wormwood, and lavender and grind together. Combine this blend in a one-to-one ratio with your weed.

Smoke a bowl and then refill. On your second bowlful, pull the smoke into the bong, filling it completely and thickly, but do not inhale. Cover the mouth hole so the smoke does not escape.

Stare deeply into the smoke, moving the bong around to change your point of view as necessary. What do you see in the smoke?

AUGUST 25
MEDITATION MOJO

Get into a meditative high and position. Think about what you like and love about yourself. What are your best qualities? How do you apply these qualities to your practice? Journal after your meditation.

AUGUST 26
HERBAL BLENDS

Create this blend to boost your creativity.

You will need:

- Mugwort (dried)
- Wormwood (dried)
- Sakae naa leaf (dried)
- Peppermint (dried)
- Blue vervain (dried)

Combine equal amounts of each herb. As you combine and grind your herbs together, focus on infusing the blend with creative intention and energy.

Combine with your weed in a one-to-one ratio. Use before and during your work as you like. This blend can be smoked or used as tea.

Add this recipe, how it feels, and your results to your Book of Shadows. If you desire, adjust ratios for flavor.

AUGUST 27
FIND YOUR WILD

Connect to the night sky with a good high. You do not have to see the stars with your physical eyes if you picture them in your mind's eye. A galaxy map can show you where you are in relation to constellations and the moon to help you get your bearings and give you images to visualize.

Stand outside in the dark with your face to the sky. Either stare into space, taking in everything you can see—the stars, the moon, even satellites and airplanes cutting across the sky—or if it is too cloudy or your view is disrupted by light pollution, picture them in your mind. The energies of air and celestial bodies are all around you. How do these energies feel to you? How do you differentiate them from one another? How can you best utilize them? Add this information to your BOS.

This exercise will be done monthly throughout the year because as the night sky changes, the energies you feel will also change.

AUGUST 28
MAGICAL MUSICAL MOVEMENT

Start a playlist of songs that boost your creativity. This playlist can be used when you want to add to your prepping and spell-work or build a creative setting for meditation or other workings. Frequency-based music may help increase creativity.

Try out your playlist by getting high and choosing a few songs to move to in whatever type of movement you prefer, even if it is only rocking back and forth. Move to the music to connect with its energy.

Try listening to your playlist motionless with your eyes closed or with a blindfold to block out other distractions. Use headphones if possible. Does it create the energy and creativity you desired?

AUGUST 29
INTRIGUING INCANTATIONS

Boost your creativity with this call for assistance. Light up your weed and say:

> I call on the muses,
> As I float higher,

My imagination grows,
With creative fire.

Use this chant on its own or with other spellwork.

AUGUST 30
DELIGHTFUL DABBLING

Create this banishing spell jar to rid something from your life. You will need to bury this jar, so keep that in mind as you choose your vessel.

You will need:

- Glass jar with lid or corked vial
- Cloves
- Frankincense
- Mistletoe
- Myrrh
- Nettle
- Black peppercorns
- Crushed red pepper
- Thistle
- Hyssop
- Cannabis ash

- Small piece of paper
- Writing instrument
- Black sealing wax
- Enough black twine to wrap around the top of your jar and tie on a charm
- "X" charm
- Cannabis incense (optional for nonsmokers)

Smoke your weed (or use another consumption method, allowing time for edibles to take effect).

Place each ingredient into your chosen jar (or mix them in a bowl and then transfer them to your jar), focusing on each one's energy along with what it is you are wanting to banish from your life. See your life without this element in it.

As you work with each ingredient, say:

I call upon the energies of [ingredient name],
Take this [focus on what you want banished] from my life.

Write on a piece of paper what it is you are banishing from your life and place it in the jar.

Take a hit (or deep, centered, intention-filled breath if you do not smoke or vape) and use your exhalation to gently blow your hopes and objectives into your jar. (You may also use the smoke from cannabis incense.)

Close the top of the jar and cover it with the melted sealing wax. Wrap the string around the jar top and attach the charm. When finished, say:

> *Take from my sight what I wish not to see.*
> *Take from my life what I wish not to be.*
> *What I wrote down, remove from my life.*
> *Banish the things I put inside.*

Bury the jar as deep as you can in a safe place where there is no danger of it being disturbed.

AUGUST 31
SOULFUL SEARCHING

Reflect on the previous month. What did you create this past month? How have you added creativity to your practice? How can you use your creativity to nourish and fuel your spirituality and Craft? Meditate and journal on your overall experiences.

September

September is the time of harvesting. Nature's fruits are ripening, and we gather in our prosperity. This month, focus on achieving prosperity in different areas of your life. Gather in your own harvest.

September Supply List

September 2

   6 × 6-inch square piece of blue material

   Agate (stone or chips)

   Maple (dried leaves, shavings, small sticks)

   Dill (dried or oil)

   Dried: red clover, sweet woodruff, blessed thistle, cinquefoil

   6 inches of gold string

   Cannabis incense (optional for nonsmokers)

September 5

   Glass jar with lid or corked vial

   Dried: jasmine, rose petals, blue lotus petals, motherwort, lavender, chamomile, catnip, damiana, lemon balm, hops, cannabis

   Blue lace agate chips

   Gray sealing wax

   Green sealing wax

   Pink sealing wax

   Enough silver string to wrap around the top of your jar and tie on a charm

   Charm such as a peace sign, dove, or other symbol

September 8

Your water charger

Lavender

Lemon balm

Citrine

Rose quartz

Clear quartz

September 14

Cannabis incense (optional for nonsmokers)

September 15

Green aventurine

September 16

Wild lettuce

September 17

Dried or fresh: basil, blessed thistle, dill, cannabis

September 18

Glass jar with lid or corked vial

Cannabis ash

Dried: pine, rosemary

Cloves

Black peppercorns

Paper

Writing instrument

Black sealing wax

September 19

Vetiver

September 20

Tea bag or strainer

Bergamot

Chamomile

Red clover

Sweet woodruff

September 24

Cannabis incense (optional for nonsmokers)

September 26

Dried: bergamot, chamomile, hops, blue vervain,
jasmine

SEPTEMBER 1
LIT LITERATURE

There is no doubt cannabis has a huge future in the United States. Research into medical applications reveals more every day. While books on this topic may be rare, you will be able to find plenty of articles from different periodicals.

Use the keywords "cannabis future" in your search to find titles of interest. This will also help you find newspaper articles. If you want to specify your search, try adding keywords such as "uses," "medical," "strains," and "production" depending on where your main interests lie. What do you want to know about the future of cannabis?

SEPTEMBER 2
TEMPTING TALISMAN

This spell jar will help draw prosperity to you. Create it now to store in your magical cupboard for later use.

You will need:

- 6 × 6-inch square piece of blue material
- Agate (stone or chips)
- Maple (dried leaves, shavings, small sticks)

- Dill (dried or oil)

- Red clover (dried)

- Sweet woodruff (dried)

- Blessed thistle (dried)

- Cinquefoil (dried)

- 6 inches of gold string

- Cannabis incense (optional for nonsmokers)

Smoke your weed (or use another consumption method) while you assemble your ingredients and create this talisman. If you have room to work at your altar, do so, or create another sacred space where you have room and are comfortable.

Lay the blue square on your altar or other stable location. Begin with the largest ingredients you are working with, most likely your stone in this instance. Add it to the center of the material.

Next, add any smaller dried herbs or flowers. Top these off with one drop of any essential oil you use. Drip it onto a dried herb or flower so it soaks into those instead of the material.

When you are done filling it, bunch the material up into a pouch and wrap the string around the neck three times before knotting it off.

Use this chant to help guide your intentions and work:

In this talisman
Powers combine,

To draw in prosperity,
Increase what is mine.

Take a hit and release your intention and exhale your smoke all over the pouch. (You may also use the smoke from cannabis incense along with your own breath.)

Store your talisman on your altar or in another magical, safe space. When you need to call upon its magic, repeat the above and add:

I call on it now,
To boost my power.
Help me fulfill,
My needs this hour.

Carry your talisman with you after activating it, place it in a prominent location in your home, or place it near something that relates to the prosperity you seek.

SEPTEMBER 3
SOULFUL SEARCHING

Parasailing, traveling the world, or reading a delightful book—what is your idea of adventure? How do you define it? What kind of adventures do you enjoy? How does your sense of adventure play a role in your spiritual practice?

SEPTEMBER 4
ASTROLOGICAL HOUSES

Research the meaning of the astrological ninth house and explore the role it plays in your life within your own chart. The ninth house represents travel and adventure. Record the information you learn and how it relates to your sign and yourself in your Book of Shadows or a journal.

SEPTEMBER 5
DELIGHTFUL DABBLING

Create this spell jar for peace of mind to keep on hand for when you need a break from mundane worries.

You will need:

- Glass jar with lid or corked vial
- Jasmine (dried)
- Rose petals (dried)
- Blue lotus petals (dried)
- Motherwort (dried)
- Lavender (dried)
- Chamomile (dried)

- Catnip (dried)
- Damiana (dried)
- Lemon balm (dried)
- Hops (dried)
- Cannabis (dried)
- Blue lace agate chips
- Gray sealing wax
- Green sealing wax
- Pink sealing wax
- Enough silver string to wrap around the top of your jar and tie on a charm
- Charm such as a peace sign, dove, or other symbol

Smoke your weed (or use another consumption method, allowing time for edibles to take effect).

Place each ingredient into your chosen jar (or mix them in a bowl and then transfer them to your jar), focusing on each one's energy along with your intention. Visualize a bubble of peace and calmness being created around you as you build and bless your jar.

As you work with each ingredient, say:

> I call upon the energies of [ingredient name],
> Bring peace to my life, store your magic here.

Take a hit (or deep, centered, intention-filled breath if you do not smoke or vape) and use your exhalation to gently blow your hopes and objectives into your jar.

Close the top of the jar and cover it with melted sealing wax, first the gray, then the green, and, finally, the pink, allowing all three of the colors to show. Wrap the silver string around the jar top and attach the charm. When finished, say:

> *When I set you in this room,*
> *Please erase any gloom.*
> *Usher in peace, calmness, and light,*
> *Help set my mind and my heart right.*

When you need the magic of this jar, place it in a prominent location in your home, next to your bed, or in your immediate vicinity. You can also carry it on your body. Repeat the above and add:

> *Create around me an aura of peace,*
> *Negativity gone; positivity increased.*

SEPTEMBER 6
CERRIDWEN'S CAULDRON

Throughout this book you've worked with many different plants, but there are many more available to work with.

Spend this month researching herbs and other plants along with their magical correspondences. What are your favorites to use? Why? What do you always keep in your witch's cupboard? Why? Document your research and preferences in your Book of Shadows.

SEPTEMBER 7
LIFTED PERSPECTIVE

Connect with your higher self in a meditative state. Step back and look at yourself objectively; allow your walls to slip away.

Examine the boundaries you have erected in your life, both for yourself and others. Which do you have a tough time keeping? Why is this true? What can you do to reinforce these boundaries? Journal about your meditation.

SEPTEMBER 8
DELIGHTFUL DABBLING

Using your water charger, combine water and earth together in this bong water herbal infusion for emotional healing.

You will need:

- Your water charger
- Lavender

- Lemon balm
- Citrine
- Rose quartz
- Clear quartz

You may either add the lavender and lemon balm to the water to steep or place the plant matter with the citrine and quartz separate from your water but in close proximity. Use this water in your bong (or drink) to aid you in your own emotional healing.

SEPTEMBER 9
FIND YOUR WILD

Discover the history of the land where you live. What plant life is native to your area? What is endangered? What plants are invasive? What steps can you take to help conserve or restore habitat?

SEPTEMBER 10
EMBRACING THE ELEMENTS

Take advantage of the warm weather before the end of summer and spend some time immersed in water outside. Whether this means going to a local lake, river, stream, or ocean, or stepping into a bucket of moon water, find a way to experience water on your skin outside. Experiment and observe what energies you can detect. How can you use them in your practice?

SEPTEMBER 11
GROWING WITH THE GREEN MAN

Fall is almost officially here, and the changes that come with it are beginning to appear. In some climates the leaves are starting to change colors as they prepare to fall to the ground.

Take time today in your high to reflect on nature's lesson in the fall: all life ends while leaving behind evidence it once existed. What evidence of your life will you leave behind? How do you want to be remembered?

SEPTEMBER 12
SUPERNATURAL SENSES

Get high and sense the sunset. Verify what time sunset will be this evening and experience as much of it as you can, even if it means only sensing it from inside a building. What shifts in energy can you feel with the setting of the sun?

SEPTEMBER 13
RECLAIMING THE SHADOW

Journal through the following questions before getting high.

How do you show yourself compassion? Remember, self-care and compassion are not the same thing. Compassion shows sympathy, empathy, and understanding. Is this easy or difficult for you to do? What obstacles have you overcome to show yourself compassion? Where do you have the most issue giving yourself compassion? How can you improve showing compassion to yourself?

After your first run-through, add your weed, connect to your higher self, and meditate on these questions. What can you add to your answers?

SEPTEMBER 14
DANK DIVINATION

Use this tarot or oracle deck layout to seek out balance in your life as the autumnal equinox approaches.

Smoke or vape your weed and blow the smoke over the cards as you shuffle them, focusing on connecting to Spirit for this objective reading of yourself. (You may consume your cannabis in a different form and use the smoke from cannabis incense.)

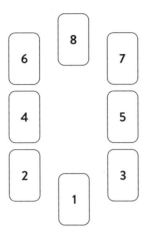

Card 1. Where I currently am.

Card 2. What throws me off balance?

Card 3. What gives me stability?

Card 4. What is my weakness?

Card 5. What is my strength?

Card 6. What is my fear?

Card 7. What is my hope?

Card 8. What guidance do I need?

Document your drawn cards and their meanings in your journal. Explore your reading in meditation.

SEPTEMBER 15
DELIGHTFUL DABBLING

Charge your weed with green aventurine to infuse it with energies for drawing money, good luck, success, and prosperity.

For a quick infusion, hold your weed (or other cannabis product) in your nondominant hand with your aventurine in your dominant hand. Move the aventurine all over and around the weed and say:

> *Send your energies from here to there,*
> *Infuse this [weed, gummy, THC, etc.]*
> *With magic's care.*
> *When it comes to the needed hour,*
> *This [weed, gummy, THC, etc.] contains aventurine's*
>   *power.*

For a deeper charge, dedicate a small box, chest, or other type of container where you can charge your cannabis by placing it, along with a green aventurine stone or chips, inside.

SEPTEMBER 16
SACRED SMOKE

Wild lettuce can be used to relieve pain and anxiety, but it also produces vivid lucid dreams.

Introduce yourself to wild lettuce by using it on its own several times first, exploring it with all your senses. How does it look? Smell? Feel? Taste? You may either smoke it or make a tealike infusion by soaking the leaves in hot water to drink.

How does it affect you? What do you feel when using it? How long does it take to feel the effects? How long do the effects last?

Evaluate and learn how wild lettuce works with your body and mind. Document this information in your Book of Shadows. Once you become familiar with this herb, combine it with cannabis and again explore the effects, being sure to document your results. This herb can be combined with others to create blends.

SEPTEMBER 17
KITCHEN WITCHERY

In the morning, combine the following ingredients in a pot of water to simmer throughout the day. Use this to draw prosperity into your life.

You will need:

- ½ teaspoon basil (dried or fresh)
- 1 teaspoon blessed thistle (dried or fresh)
- 2 teaspoons dill (dried or fresh)
- Pinch of cannabis (dried or fresh)

As you prepare the ingredients and add them to the pot, pour intention into your work. Focus on drawing prosperity into your life.

Keep the pot on a low flame on a back burner. Stir the pot nine times clockwise once every hour throughout the day.

Each time you stir the pot, say:

Fire, water, earth, and air,
My magic has a little flare.
Fruits from the earth simmer for me,
Summon energies of prosperity.

Add more water as needed to replenish what has evaporated. At the end of the day, pour the remains outside on the ground near a tree or under a bush. Return the plant material to the earth it came from. Add this recipe to your BOS and record your own experience with it.

SEPTEMBER 18
DELIGHTFUL DABBLING

This is a symbolic binding spell to help you set something aside to deal with at a different time in the future. When you are overwhelmed with something, this is the place to stick it until you are ready to deal with it.

You will need:

- Glass jar with lid or corked vial
- Cannabis ash
- Pine (dried)
- Rosemary (dried)
- Cloves
- Black peppercorns
- Paper
- Writing instrument
- Black sealing wax

Smoke your weed (or use another consumption method, allowing time for edibles to take effect).

Place each ingredient into your chosen jar (or mix them in a bowl and then transfer them to your jar), focusing on each one's energy along with your intention. Visualize a protective bubble being created around you as you build and bless your jar. Whatever you place inside of this jar will be kept here until you release it. Think of it as a lockbox, and you are the only key.

As you work with each ingredient, say:

> *I call upon the energies of [ingredient name],*
> *Create here a barrier; neutralize what I place inside.*

Write on a piece of paper a brief description of what it is you are binding and place it in the jar.

Take a hit (or deep, centered, intention-filled breath if you do not smoke or vape) and use your exhalation to gently blow your hopes and objectives into your jar.

Close the top of the jar and cover it with the melted black sealing wax. When finished, say:

> *Into this jar, I do place,*
> *That which I need out of my face.*
> *I bind it here to set aside,*
> *'Til its time comes, here it will bide.*

When you are ready to unbind what is in the jar, peel off the wax and burn the contents.

SEPTEMBER 19
ETHEREAL ESSENCES

Research the different correspondences and uses associated with vetiver and add a supply to your witch's cupboard. Add the information you find to your BOS. Dried vetiver can be smoked, combined with cannabis, or made into a tea. Meet the essence of vetiver in the following meditative practice.

Get into an elevated high and comfortable position with a small container of dried vetiver, a bottle of oil, or incense lit and placed in front of you.

Close your eyes and take several deep breaths. Allow your mind to settle and focus. When you are ready, pick up the vetiver and hold it about four inches away from your nose. Inhale the scent, breathing deeply. If it's not too overpowering for you, move it closer. Some people have sensitivities, so don't feel you have to move it directly under your nose. Oils are very potent and do not need to be moved as close.

How does this scent make you feel? Is it pleasing? Irritating? Relaxing? Exciting? Powerful? Meditate on the feelings it evokes in you.

Journal about your experience. If you feel the need to clear the scent from your nose, sniff coffee beans or grounds to help neutralize the scent.

SEPTEMBER 20
HERBAL INFUSIONS

Combine water and earth together in this bong water herbal infusion to draw prosperity.

You will need:

- Tea bag or strainer
- Bergamot
- Chamomile
- Red clover
- Sweet woodruff

Use this water in your bong or drink it as tea.

SEPTEMBER 21
VIBING

Experiment with the following types of frequency-based music to see how they affect you.

- 396 Hz activates the root chakra and helps to assuage fear and allow the listener to feel liberated.
- 417 Hz activates the sacral chakra and helps to resolve past traumas and bring about change.

- 528 Hz activates the solar plexus chakra and assists in transformations.

Use a search engine or music service to find music in these different frequencies to listen to, preferably with headphones. Get high to experience how these frequencies feel to you. Journal about your experience.

SEPTEMBER 22
SOULFUL SEARCHING

In a meditative state, search through your mental inventory of fictional witches you are familiar with. Select a couple or few you admire. What do you admire about these characters? How have they been influential to you? Journal about how these witches have inspired you.

SEPTEMBER 23
RECLAIMING THE SHADOW

Get high, connect with your higher self or power, and meditate on what you like about yourself. What are your favorite aspects of you? Make a list of your top three favorite traits about yourself in your journal.

SEPTEMBER 24
DANK DIVINATION

Grab a small tray, plate, or bowl along with your grinder and a bud. Place the bud in the grinder and grind it. Smoke or vape your weed, and as you exhale, gently blow the smoke across your grinder. (You may also use the smoke from cannabis incense.) Focus on opening your mind to receive images through the ground bud. Dump the bud out onto your tray, plate, or bowl. Watch how the weed moves and settles into place. What messages can you find? Record your experience in your Book of Shadows.

SEPTEMBER 25
MEDITATION MOJO

Slip into a meditative state in a comfortable position and contemplate your own capabilities. What are your strengths? What are your weaknesses? How do each of these affect your spirituality? Journal about your meditation.

SEPTEMBER 26
HERBAL BLENDS

Create this blend to boost your prosperity.

You will need:

- Bergamot (dried)
- Chamomile (dried)
- Hops (dried)
- Blue vervain (dried)
- Jasmine (dried)

Combine equal amounts of the herbs. As you combine and grind them together, focus on infusing the blend with prosperous intention and energy. Combine with your weed in a one-to-one ratio. This blend can be smoked or used as tea. Use this blend on its own for a boost or to accompany your prosperity-themed spellwork.

Add this recipe, how it feels, and your results to your Book of Shadows. If you desire, adjust ratios for flavor.

SEPTEMBER 27
FIND YOUR WILD

Connect to the night sky with a good high. You do not have to see the stars with your physical eyes if you picture them in your mind's eye. A galaxy map can show you where you are in relation to constellations and the moon to help you get your bearings and give you images to visualize.

Stand outside in the dark with your face to the sky. Either stare into space, taking in everything you can see—the stars, the moon, even satellites and airplanes cutting across the sky— or if it is too cloudy or your view is disrupted by light pollution, picture them in your mind. The energies of air and celestial bodies are all around you. How do these energies feel to you? How do you differentiate them from one another? How can you best utilize them? Add this information to your BOS.

This exercise will be done monthly throughout the year because as the night sky changes, the energies you feel will also change.

SEPTEMBER 28
MAGICAL MUSICAL MOVEMENT

Start a playlist of songs to draw in energies of prosperity. This playlist can be used when you want to add to your prepping and spellwork or build a creative setting for meditation or other workings. Be sure to check out frequency-based music.

Try out your playlist by getting high and choosing a few songs to move to in whatever type of movement you prefer, even if it is only rocking back and forth.

Try listening to your playlist motionless with your eyes closed or with a blindfold to block out other distractions. Use headphones if possible. Does it create the energy and environment you desire?

SEPTEMBER 29
INTRIGUING INCANTATIONS

Increase your prosperity with this chant:

> *What I need, bring to me,*
> *Rich in abundant prosperity.*
> *What I desire, bring to me,*
> *Rich in abundant prosperity.*

Use this chant alone or with other spellwork. Be sure to add it to your BOS.

SEPTEMBER 30
SOULFUL SEARCHING

What type of prosperity did you work to bring into your life this month? What success did you find in your workings? Where else do you need to focus your attention to be more prosperous? Meditate and journal on your overall experiences and how they contributed to your practice, spirituality, or both.

October

October is the first full month of the season when darkness has overtaken the light. As the veil between worlds thins, the theme of protection becomes popular. This month, you will focus on diverse ways to add energetic spiritual protection to your practice.

October Supply List
October 2

>2 pieces of 6 × 6-inch square black material (felt or another thicker material)
>
>Obsidian stone or chips
>
>Hawthorn thorns
>
>Blackberry thorns

Raspberry thorns

Brambles

Buckthorn thorns

Thistles

Chili or other hot pepper (dried or oil)

Pieces of cracked walnut shells

Small piece of oak (wood or bark)

Black pepper

Cedar shavings

Burdock burrs

Cloves

Dried: blue vervain, cinnamon, California poppy, hyssop, mugwort, mullein

6 inches of black ribbon

Cannabis incense (optional for nonsmokers)

October 5

Glass jar with lid or corked vial

Dried: mugwort, mullein, hyssop, broom, wormwood

Cloves (or clove oil)

Peppercorns

Obsidian chips

Clear quartz chips

Cannabis ash

Black sealing wax

Enough black twine to wrap around the top of
your jar and tie on a charm

Pentagram or other sign of protection

October 8

Your water charger

Clear quartz

Obsidian

Cinnamon

Clove

October 12

Variety of stones you can identify by sight

October 14

Cannabis incense (optional for nonsmokers)

October 16

California poppy

October 17

Small piece of oak (wood or bark)

Thorns from a hawthorn tree

Black pepper

Cedar shavings

Burdock burrs

Whole cloves

Fresh or dried: blue vervain, cannabis

October 18

Obsidian

October 19

Black pepper

October 20

Tea bag or strainer

Ground cinnamon (or 1 stick)

Cloves

October 22

Glass jar with lid or corked vial

Frankincense resin

Dried: grape leaves, ivy, violets, lotus, myrrh, worm-wood, cannabis

Cannabis ash

Amethyst chips

Obsidian chips

Paper

Writing instrument

Black sealing wax

Blue sealing wax

Orange sealing wax

Purple sealing wax

October 24

2 black candles

Lighter

Paper

Writing instrument

Cannabis incense (optional for nonsmokers)

October 26

Dried: mugwort, mullein, hyssop

OCTOBER 1
LIT LITERATURE

Spirit communication is greatly enhanced with the use of cannabis. Learn about developing and advancing this skill as the veil thins this month.

No matter where you shop for books, use the keywords "spirit communication" in your search to find titles of interest.

OCTOBER 2
TEMPTING TALISMAN

Create this protection talisman to carry on your person to create a protective bubble around you.

- 2 pieces of 6 × 6-inch square black material (felt or another thicker material)
- Obsidian stone or chips
- Hawthorn thorns
- Blackberry thorns
- Raspberry thorns
- Brambles
- Buckthorn thorns

- Thistles
- Chili or other hot pepper (dried or oil)
- Pieces of cracked walnut shells
- Small piece of oak (wood or bark)
- Black pepper
- Cedar shavings
- Burdock burrs
- Cloves
- Blue vervain (dried)
- Cinnamon (dried)
- California poppy (dried)
- Hyssop (dried)
- Mugwort (dried)
- Mullein (dried)
- 6 inches of black ribbon
- Cannabis incense (optional for nonsmokers)

Smoke your weed (or use another consumption method) while you assemble your ingredients and create this talisman. If you have room to work at your altar, do so, or create another sacred space where you have room and are comfortable.

Lay the black square on your altar or other stable location with the second piece on top of it. You will double it up due to all the pokey thorns you will be working with. Begin with the largest ingredients you are working with, most likely your stones in this instance. Add them to the center of the material.

Next, add any smaller dried herbs or flowers. Top these off with one drop of any essential oils you use. Drip them onto a dried herb or flower so they soak into those instead of the material.

When you are done filling it, bunch the material up into a pouch and wrap the ribbon around the neck three times before knotting it off.

Use this chant to help guide your intentions and work:

> *Protect my spirit, mind, and body.*
> *Keep me safe,*
> *Create a barrier around me.*

Take a hit and release your intention and exhale your smoke all over the pouch. (You may also use the smoke from cannabis incense along with your own breath.)

Store your talisman on your altar or in another magical, safe space. Carry it with you when you desire its magic.

OCTOBER 3
SOULFUL SEARCHING

Get high for this exercise and document this information about yourself in your Book of Shadows. This month's astrological house represents your work life and career. What are your own views on this area in your life? Detail your work ethic or philosophy. How did you form these beliefs? Who and what influenced you and how?

OCTOBER 4
ASTROLOGICAL HOUSES

Research the meaning of the astrological tenth house and explore the role it plays in your life within your own chart. The tenth house represents your work life and career. Record the information you learn and how it relates to your sign and yourself in your Book of Shadows or a journal.

OCTOBER 5
DELIGHTFUL DABBLING

Create this spell jar for a second layer of protection. While you can carry your talisman with you, this jar will generate an aura of protection in the room, throughout your home, or wherever you set your focus.

You will need:

- Glass jar with lid or corked vial
- Mugwort (dried)
- Mullein (dried)
- Hyssop (dried)
- Broom (dried)
- Wormwood (dried)
- Cloves (or clove oil)
- Peppercorns
- Obsidian chips
- Clear quartz chips
- Cannabis ash
- Black sealing wax
- Enough black twine to wrap around the top of your jar and tie on a charm
- Pentagram or other sign of protection

Smoke your weed (or use another consumption method, allowing time for edibles to take effect).

Place each ingredient into your chosen jar (or mix them in a bowl and then transfer them to your jar), focusing on each one's energy along with your intention. Visualize a protective bubble being created around you as you build and bless your jar.

As you work with each ingredient, say:

I call upon the energies of [ingredient name],
Protect me and my home.
Protect me and my space.

Take a hit (or deep, centered, intention-filled breath if you do not smoke or vape) and use your exhalation to gently blow your hopes and objectives into your jar.

Close the top of the jar and cover it with the melted sealing wax. Wrap the black twine around the jar top and attach the charm. When finished, say:

Protect me and my home.
Protect me and my place.
Create all around me,
A protective safe space.

Place the jar on your altar or in a prominent location in your home where it can disperse its protective energy.

OCTOBER 6
CERRIDWEN'S CAULDRON

Research the history of Spiritualism to discover its impact on witchcraft today. While certain aspects of Spiritualism have grown with the witchcraft community, other aspects were ripe with fraud. Focus on learning to separate the truth from fiction.

No matter where you shop for books, use the keywords "Spiritualism," "Spiritualist," or "the history of Spiritualism" in your search to find books of interest.

OCTOBER 7
LIFTED PERSPECTIVE

Connect with your higher self in a meditative state. Step back and look at yourself objectively; allow your walls to slip away.

Focus on the following affirmation:

> *I shift my mind from passively waiting*
> *To a new perspective of actively creating.*

How does this affirmation apply to your life? What does it mean to you? Journal about your meditation.

OCTOBER 8
DELIGHTFUL DABBLING

Using your water charger, combine water and earth together in this bong water herbal infusion for protection.

You will need:

- Your water charger
- Clear quartz
- Obsidian
- Cinnamon
- Clove

You may either add the cinnamon and clove to the water to steep or place the plant matter with the obsidian and quartz separate from your water but in close proximity. Use this water in your bong (or drink) for a protective boost before workings.

OCTOBER 9
FIND YOUR WILD

Find a place to take a nature break today and seek out the natural energies of fall. After you get high, spend at least fifteen minutes outside, preferably in a location with as few other people and distractions as possible. Close your eyes and tune out all human-caused energies around you. Eliminate manufactured sounds and scents. Allow yourself several minutes to adjust to the energies around you and shuffle through them, marking those you can for ignoring. What natural forces can you detect? What do you hear? What do you smell? What do you feel in the air?

OCTOBER 10
EMBRACING THE ELEMENTS

Using actual earth for grounding can be difficult for some people for several reasons: (1) Inner city locations do not have as much access to natural dirt or earthy areas. (2) Physical limitations may make it inaccessible. (3) Inclement weather, including cold and snow, can be a hindrance.

Creating a grounding travel kit brings the earth to you when you cannot go to it. Collect a variety of soil, salt, sand, small pebbles, or clay in containers to stock your witch's cupboard. What differences do you detect in their signature energies?

OCTOBER 11
GROWING WITH THE GREEN MAN

Learn about plant life you can forage in your area and how to identify it, along with each plant's magical and medicinal uses.

Where can you safely search for plants to forage? Document your hunting grounds and what you collect at each location in your Book of Shadows.

OCTOBER 12
SUPERNATURAL SENSES

Place a variety of stones and crystals into a non-see-through bag. Something like a drawstring tarot deck bag would work great. Reach your hand into the bag without looking and select a stone. Hold it in your hand but keep it in the bag so there is no chance of you seeing it with your eyes. Metaphysically listen to the stone in your hand. What are its characteristics? Sense the information from the stone. Guess which stone it is and then check to see if you are correct. Begin this exercise using four or five stones. As you become more familiar with their different energies, increase the number of stones.

OCTOBER 13
RECLAIMING THE SHADOW

Connect with your higher self in deep meditation. What emotions do you hide behind a mask? What do you find difficult to feel or express? Ask yourself why you feel this way. When you have an answer, continue asking why until you come to the core of the problem. How do you cope (or not cope) when dealing with this feeling? What can you do now to change how you express this feeling? Journal about your experience.

OCTOBER 14
DANK DIVINATION

Smoke or vape your weed and blow the smoke over your tarot or oracle cards as you shuffle them, focusing on receiving messages from higher spirits. (You may consume your cannabis in a different form and use the smoke from cannabis incense.)

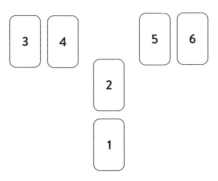

Card 1. Yourself in your current situation.

Card 2. Message from your higher self.

Card 3. Message from a departed loved one.

Card 4. Message from an ancestor.

Card 5. Message from your spirit guide.

Card 6. Message from your higher power.

Document your drawn cards and their meanings in your journal. Explore your reading in meditation.

OCTOBER 15
SOULFUL SEARCHING

In a meditative state, search through your mental inventory of other real witches you are familiar with. These may be friends or family as well as more "famous" witches such as activists, authors, or social media influencers. Select a few you admire. What do you admire about these people? How have they been influential to you? Journal about how these witches have inspired you.

OCTOBER 16
SACRED SMOKE

California poppy is used for pain relief and calmness and produces a light high. Used with cannabis, the two increase the effects of the other.

Introduce yourself to California poppy by using it on its own several times first, exploring it with all your senses. How does it look? Smell? Feel? Taste? You may either smoke it or make a tealike infusion by soaking the leaves in hot water to drink.

How does it affect you? What do you feel when using it? How long does it take to feel the effects? How long do the effects last?

Evaluate and learn how California poppy works with your body and mind. Document this information in your Book of Shadows. Once you become familiar with this herb, combine it with cannabis and again explore the effects, being sure to document your results. This herb can be combined with others to create blends.

OCTOBER 17
KITCHEN WITCHERY

In the morning, combine the following ingredients in a pot of water to simmer throughout the day. Use this on days when you want to boost your protection. Be sure to start your simmer pot early so it has time to simmer and get the energies and magic started around you.

You will need:

- Small piece of oak (wood or bark)
- 3 thorns from a hawthorn tree
- ½ teaspoon black pepper
- ¼ cup cedar shavings
- 9 burdock burrs
- 9 whole cloves
- 1 tablespoon blue vervain (fresh or dried)
- Pinch of cannabis (fresh or dried)

As you prepare the ingredients and add them to the pot, pour intention into your work. Focus on building protective walls around yourself and your home.

Keep the pot on a low flame on a back burner. Stir the pot nine times clockwise once every hour throughout the day.

Each time you stir the pot, say:

> *Fire, water, earth, and air,*
> *Fruits from the earth simmer here.*
> *Walls surround me, keep me safe,*
> *Protect me and my sacred space.*

Add more water as needed to replenish what has evaporated. At the end of the day, pour the remains outside on the ground near a tree or under a bush. Return the plant material to the earth it came from. Add this recipe to your BOS and record your own experience with it.

OCTOBER 18
DELIGHTFUL DABBLING

Charge your weed with obsidian to infuse it with energies to absorb negativity, provide protection, and aid in spirit communication.

For a quick infusion, hold your weed (or other cannabis product) in your nondominant hand with your obsidian in your dominant hand. Move the obsidian all over and around the weed and say:

> *Send your energies from here to there,*
> *Infuse this [weed, gummy, THC, etc.]*
> *With magic's care.*

When it comes to the needed hour,
This [weed, gummy, THC, etc.] contains obsidian's power.

For a deeper charge, dedicate a small box, chest, or other type of container where you can charge your cannabis by placing it, along with an obsidian stone or chips, inside.

OCTOBER 19
ETHEREAL ESSENCES

Research the different correspondences and uses associated with black pepper and add a supply to your witch's cupboard. Add the information you find to your BOS. Dried peppercorns can be ground to smoke (you only need a little!), combined with cannabis, or used whole to make into a tea. Meet the essence of black pepper in the following meditative practice.

Get into an elevated high and comfortable position with a small container of peppercorns, a bottle of oil, or incense lit and placed in front of you.

Close your eyes and take several deep breaths. Allow your mind to settle and focus. When you are ready, pick up the black pepper and hold it about ten inches away from your nose. Inhale the scent, breathing deeply. If it's not too overpowering for you, move it closer. Some people have sensitivities, so don't feel you have to move it directly under your nose. Oils are very potent and do not need to be moved as close. Don't be surprised if you sneeze.

How does this scent make you feel? Is it pleasing? Irritating? Relaxing? Exciting? Powerful? Meditate on the feelings it evokes in you.

Journal about your experience. If you feel the need to clear the scent from your nose, sniff coffee beans or grounds to help neutralize the scent.

OCTOBER 20
HERBAL INFUSIONS

Combine water and earth together in this bong water herbal infusion for protection.

You will need:

- Tea bag or strainer
- 2 teaspoons ground cinnamon (or 1 stick)
- 3 cloves

Use this water in your bong or drink it as tea. Add this recipe to your Book of Shadows and record your own experience with it.

OCTOBER 21
VIBING

Experiment with the following types of frequency-based music to see how they affect you.

- 852 Hz helps to awaken your intuition and activates the third eye chakra.

- 963 Hz, known as the "God frequency," activates the crown chakra and helps you to connect to the Divine.

Use a search engine or music service to find music in these different frequencies to listen to, preferably with headphones. Get high to experience how these frequencies feel to you. Journal about your experience.

OCTOBER 22
DELIGHTFUL DABBLING

This spell jar for transformation is to help you make the changes you want in your life, such as breaking old habits or boosting your success in starting new ones. Transform your life to the life you want it to be.

You will need:

- Glass jar with lid or corked vial
- Frankincense resin
- Grape leaves (dried)
- Ivy (dried)
- Violets (dried)
- Lotus (dried)
- Myrrh (dried)
- Wormwood (dried)
- Cannabis (dried)
- Cannabis ash
- Amethyst chips
- Obsidian chips
- Paper
- Writing instrument
- Black sealing wax
- Blue sealing wax
- Orange sealing wax
- Purple sealing wax

Smoke your weed (or use another consumption method, allowing time for edibles to take effect).

Place each ingredient into your chosen jar (or mix them in a bowl and then transfer them to your jar), focusing on each one's energy along with your intention.

As you work with each ingredient, say:

I call upon the energies of [ingredient name],
Help me to transform my life.

Write down the transformation you seek on a piece of paper and place it in the jar.

Take a hit (or deep, centered, intention-filled breath if you do not smoke or vape) and use your exhalation to gently blow your hopes and objectives into your jar.

Close the top of the jar and cover it with the melted sealing wax, allowing all the colors to be shown. Start with black, then blue, then orange, and finish with purple. When finished, say:

This change I invite,
With magic's power
And energy's might,
To transform my life anew.
Make this change for me come true.

Carry the spell jar on you or place it in a prominent location in your home.

OCTOBER 23
RECLAIMING THE SHADOW

Baked is great, burnt out is not. Answer these questions in your journal before getting high: Where have you suffered from burnout in your life? How do you express mental exhaustion? What symptoms and signs do you suffer from when burnout is hitting? How do you recover? After answering, get into a relaxed high and reward yourself with a gentle chill.

OCTOBER 24
DANK DIVINATION

Use your high to boost your psychic abilities and try your hand at automatic writing.

You will need:

- 2 black candles
- Lighter
- Paper
- Writing instrument
- Cannabis incense (optional for nonsmokers)

In a dark or dimly lit room, light two black candles and place them about twelve inches in front of you, about ten inches apart. Place your paper in front of you. Music can be extremely helpful in distracting your mind and allowing you to zone out instead of paying attention to what your hand wants to write. Use frequency-based or instrumental music so you aren't accidentally writing out lyrics.

Smoke or vape your weed, and as you exhale, gently blow the smoke over the paper and your chosen writing instrument, as well as in between the two candles, while opening your mind. (You can use cannabis incense and your own breath if you are a nonsmoker.) Begin by circling your writing instrument on the paper and let your higher self take over.

Record your experience in your Book of Shadows along with any information you obtain through research on automatic writing.

OCTOBER 25
MEDITATION MOJO

Get into a comfortable position and slip into a meditative high and contemplate what makes you feel valued. What makes you feel validated? How does this affect your spiritual path? Journal about your meditation.

OCTOBER 26
HERBAL BLENDS

Create this blend to boost your spiritual protection.

You will need:

- Mugwort (dried)
- Mullein (dried)
- Hyssop (dried)

Begin by combining equal amounts of the dried herbs together. As you combine and grind your herbs, focus on infusing the blend with protective intention and energy. Combine with your weed in a one-to-one ratio. Dust with a sprinkling of ground cloves and ground cinnamon. This blend can be smoked or used as tea. Use this blend on its own for a boost or to accompany any of your workings.

Add this recipe, how it feels, and your results to your Book of Shadows. If you desire, adjust ratios for flavor.

OCTOBER 27
FIND YOUR WILD

Connect to the night sky with a good high. You do not have to see the stars with your physical eyes if you picture them in your mind's eye. A galaxy map can show you where you are in relation to constellations and the moon to help you get your bearings and give you images to visualize.

Stand outside in the dark with your face to the sky. Either stare into space, taking in everything you can see—the stars, the moon, even satellites and airplanes cutting across the sky— or if it is too cloudy or your view is disrupted by light pollution, picture them in your mind. The energies of air and celestial bodies are all around you. How do these energies feel to you? How do you differentiate them from one another? How can you best utilize them? Add this information to your BOS.

This exercise will be done monthly throughout the year because as the night sky changes, the energies you feel will also change.

OCTOBER 28
MAGICAL MUSICAL MOVEMENT

Start a playlist of songs that help tune you in to the spirit realm for communication with those beyond the veil. This playlist can be used during your spirit communication or divination sessions, along with during prep and spellwork or other workings. Be sure to check out frequency-based music, which may help you connect with the spirit world.

Try out your playlist by getting high and choosing a few songs to move to in whatever type of movement you prefer, even if it is only rocking back and forth.

Try listening to your playlist motionless with your eyes closed or with a blindfold to block out other distractions. Use headphones if possible. Does it create the energy and environment you desire?

OCTOBER 29
INTRIGUING INCANTATIONS

Create a safe space for yourself with these words of protection:

> *By the air, the water, earth, and fire,*
> *Protection is the blessing I desire.*
> *Keep me comfortable, safe, and sound,*
> *This is my wish; my words be bound.*

This simple protection chant can be used by itself or added to any other spellwork.

OCTOBER 30
SOULFUL SEARCHING

How have you added protection to your practice this month? What makes you feel unsafe? What makes you feel safe? How does your perception of your safety affect your spirituality? Meditate and journal your responses.

OCTOBER 31
MEDITATION MOJO

On this night of costumes and creatures, enjoy your high with a playful sesh of make believe. Have fun as you let your mind wander in meditation and imagine what your life would be like if you lived as a costumed character of your choosing.

November

It is the time for energies to turn inward, so November is the perfect time to work on communication, both your internal communication and how you choose to communicate with others.

November Supply List
November 2

> 6 × 6-inch square piece of blue material
>
> Quartz
>
> Dried: willow leaf, orris root
>
> Rose petals (dried or oil)

6 inches of blue ribbon

Cannabis incense (optional for nonsmokers)

November 5

1 corked vial for each person

Dried: chamomile, daisy petals, dandelion leaves, marigold petals, rosemary, cannabis

Allspice (whole or ground)

Tiger's eye (stone or a few chips)

Clear quartz (stone or a few chips)

Blue sealing wax

Yellow sealing wax

November 8

Glass jar with lid or corked vial

Small piece of paper

Writing instrument

Dried: clover, garlic, lilac, marjoram, mugwort, rice, vanilla bean

Hematite chips

Quartz chips

Cannabis

Green sealing wax

Enough yellow twine to wrap around the top of
   your jar and tie on a charm

Charm that represents community to you: bee, hive,
   fish, etc.

November 10

Cannabis incense (optional for nonsmokers)

November 12

Set of runes

November 14

Cannabis incense (optional for nonsmokers)

November 15

Moonstone

November 16

Sakae naa leaf

November 17

Maple syrup

Whole allspice

Dried or fresh: chamomile, marigold petals, sacred lotus petals, cannabis

November 19

Turmeric

November 20

Dried: chamomile, dandelion, jasmine, lavender

November 24

2 black candles

Lighter

Casting bones

Cannabis incense (optional for nonsmokers)

November 26

Dried: blue lotus, chamomile, dandelion leaves, lavender, motherwort, sacred lotus, tulsi

NOVEMBER 1
LIT LITERATURE

Earlier in the year, you read about Paganism from a modern perspective, within the past ten years. It's time to turn back the clock and imagine the card catalog of fifty years ago. Choose a title that is at minimum fifty years old. Some of these books may have an updated annotated version, but many will not. It is important to not only understand history, but also to understand the full role outdated histories played while shaping and forming ideas and practices.

No matter where you shop for books, use the keywords "classic Paganism" or "classic Pagan titles" in your search to find books of interest.

NOVEMBER 2
TEMPTING TALISMAN

Create this talisman to help open your heart and mind to open and honest communication with yourself and others.

- 6 × 6-inch square piece of blue material
- Quartz
- Willow leaf (dried)

- Orris root (dried)
- Rose petals (dried or oil)
- 6 inches of blue ribbon
- Cannabis incense (optional for nonsmokers)

Smoke your weed (or use another consumption method) while you assemble your ingredients and create this talisman. If you have room to work at your altar, do so, or create another sacred space where you have room and are comfortable.

Lay the square on your altar or other stable location. Begin with the largest ingredients you are working with, most likely your stone in this instance. Add them to the center of the material.

Next, add any smaller dried herbs or flowers. Top these off with one drop of any essential oils you use. Drip them onto a dried herb or flower so they soak into those instead of the material.

When you are done filling it, bunch the material up into a pouch and wrap the ribbon around the neck three times before knotting it off.

Use this chant to help guide your intentions and work:

Open my heart,
Open my mind,
Speak my truth,
Unleash its bind.

Give strength to my voice,
To say what I need to,
Give guidance for words,
Honest and true.

Take a hit and release your intention and exhale your smoke all over the pouch. (You may also use the smoke from cannabis incense along with your own breath.)

Store your talisman on your altar or in another magical, safe space. When you need its power, activate it by repeating the chant above.

NOVEMBER 3
SOULFUL SEARCHING

Get high for this meditative journaling session. This month's astrological house represents your friendships and communities. Journal about the functions you fulfill in your close friendships and the variety of communities you participate in. What patterns do you see? What satisfaction do you find in these roles? What changes do you want to make?

NOVEMBER 4
ASTROLOGICAL HOUSES

Research the meaning of the astrological eleventh house and explore the role it plays in your life within your own chart. The eleventh house represents your friendships and community. Record the information you learn and how it relates to your sign and yourself in your Book of Shadows or a journal.

NOVEMBER 5
DELIGHTFUL DABBLING

Open the lines of communication with those you love with the aid of these magical vials. If possible, these vials should be constructed with the person or people in attendance and participating. Or one person may build and dispense them to the others, particularly if there is a great physical distance between them.

- 1 corked vial for each person
- Chamomile (dried)
- Daisy petals (dried)
- Dandelion leaves (dried)
- Marigold petals (dried)

- Rosemary (dried)
- Cannabis (dried)
- Allspice (whole or ground)
- Tiger's eye (stone or a few chips)
- Clear quartz (stone or a few chips)
- Blue sealing wax
- Yellow sealing wax

Smoke your weed (or use another consumption method, allowing time for edibles to take effect).

Place each ingredient into your chosen jar (or mix them in a bowl and then transfer them to your jar), focusing on each one's energy along with your intention. If you are working with others, take turns or work in unison.

As you work with each ingredient, say:

> I call upon the energies of [ingredient name],
> Aid us in our communication.

Take a hit (or deep, centered, intention-filled breath if you do not smoke or vape) and use your exhalation to gently blow your hopes and objectives into your jar.

Close the top of the vial and cover it with the melted blue wax, then yellow, allowing both colors to show. When finished, say:

Into this vial,
My love I pour,
For lines of communication
To be restored.
Open and honest,
And full of love,
When we speak,
Peace of the dove.

When a discussion is needed, each participant should activate their vial by repeating the above blessing.

NOVEMBER 6
CERRIDWEN'S CAULDRON

The law of conservation of energy dictates energy cannot be created or destroyed, only transformed from one form to another. This law supports the theory of reincarnation. Past-life regression is the process of going back to revisit who you were in previous incarnations.

What has been your previous experience with past-life regressions or therapy? Is there a time period from before your current lifetime you feel drawn to? Do you have an affinity for a specific location you have never visited before? There may be figments of memories from previous lives.

Get high and meditate, asking your higher self to show you a glimpse of a previous incarnation. Who, what, where, and when do you see?

Journal about your experience and add a section to your BOS to track incarnations. Work with a past-life therapist or hypnotist if desired.

NOVEMBER 7
LIFTED PERSPECTIVE

Get high for this meditative journaling session.

Hindsight is twenty-twenty. Look back at a time when you were confident in your point of view only to later learn you did not see things clearly. How does this situation look different to you now? What did you miss or misinterpret? What does this teach you about enlarging your point of view?

NOVEMBER 8
DELIGHTFUL DABBLING

This jar can be created by yourself for a community, or a community can join together to create one large jar for the group. Community members can each donate an ingredient.

You will need:

- Glass jar with lid or corked vial
- Small piece of paper
- Writing instrument
- Clover (dried)
- Garlic (dried)
- Lilac (dried)
- Marjoram (dried)
- Mugwort (dried)
- Rice (dried)
- Vanilla bean (dried)
- Hematite chips
- Quartz chips
- Cannabis
- Green sealing wax
- Enough yellow twine to wrap around the top of your jar and tie on a charm
- Charm that represents community to you: bee, hive, fish, etc.

Smoke your weed (or use another consumption method, allowing time for edibles to take effect).

Create a statement of intent for your community. What do you wish for this community? For example: To grow and maintain an interactive community centered on spirituality. Roll or fold up the paper and drop it in the bottom of the jar to cover with the other ingredients.

Place each ingredient into your chosen jar (or mix them in a bowl and then transfer them to your jar), focusing on each one's energy along with your intention.

As you work with each ingredient, say:

[I or we] call upon the energies of [ingredient name],
Combine together in this vessel,
Save [me or us] your strength.

Take a hit (or deep, centered, intention-filled breath if you do not smoke or vape) and use your exhalation to gently blow your hopes and objectives into your jar.

Close the top of the jar and cover it with the melted sealing wax. Wrap the string around the jar top and attach the charm. When finished, say:

Bless the power
Stored in this place,
Help it grow,
And protect our space.
Bless us as we come together,
Join our magic in this endeavor.

When your community has an event, place the jar in a central location to disperse and recharge its magic among your community members.

NOVEMBER 9
FIND YOUR WILD

As the United States prepares to celebrate Thanksgiving, learn the history of the land and who inhabited it before you. Research the Indigenous people who once lived their own connection with the same land. Honor them in a reflective meditation.

NOVEMBER 10
EMBRACING THE ELEMENTS

Take a step outside and smoke or vape to hit a high today. Experience and appreciate the sensation of the air as it touches your skin, especially on your face. Is it warm? Chilly? Crisp? How does it make you feel? As you smoke or vape, focus on the intake of air, and then follow the path the smoke takes as you slowly exhale. Experiment making clouds and trailing swirls. Center on where the smoke disperses into the surrounding air, disappearing before your eyes. This is the same way exhaling other energies works, diffusing them into the universe. If you do not smoke or vape, try waving a cannabis incense stick around and focus on the swirling smoke.

NOVEMBER 11
GROWING WITH THE GREEN MAN

We are in the depth of fall, the time of year when much of the plant life goes dormant and fields are fallow. The leaves have fallen from the trees and carpet the ground underneath them.

Spend time outside in a local environment where you can get high and observe the energy of the natural world around you. What do you feel? What differences can you detect comparing today to other times of the year?

NOVEMBER 12
SUPERNATURAL SENSES

Place runes into a non-see-through bag. Something like a drawstring tarot deck bag would work great. Reach your hand into the bag without looking and select one. Hold it in your hand but keep it in the bag so there is no chance of you seeing it with your eyes. Metaphysically listen to the rune in your hand. What are its characteristics? Sense the information from the rune. Guess which one it is and then check to see if you are correct. Begin this exercise using four or five runes. As you become more familiar with their different energies, increase the number used.

NOVEMBER 13
RECLAIMING THE SHADOW

Meet your higher self in a deep meditation. Think of the way you treat yourself: Would you want to be in a relationship with you? Would you be friends with a person who treats you the way you treat yourself? Would you date someone who treats you the way you treat yourself? What parts of how you treat yourself do you like? What needs to be changed and how? Journal about your experience.

NOVEMBER 14
DANK DIVINATION

Smoke or vape your weed and blow the smoke over your tarot or oracle cards as you shuffle them, focusing on your role in a chosen community you wish to explore. (You may consume your cannabis in a different form and use the smoke from cannabis incense.) Lay out eight cards in a line to read as follows:

Card 1. Your current self.

Card 2. The role you believe you play in this community.

Card 3. The role you actively play in the community.

Card 4. Strengths of your role in the community.

Card 5. Weaknesses of your role in the community.

Card 6. What you can learn from others in the community.

Card 7. What you can contribute to others in the community.

Card 8. Message from your higher self regarding your role in the community.

Document your drawn cards and their meanings in your journal. Explore your reading in meditation.

NOVEMBER 15
DELIGHTFUL DABBLING

Charge your weed with moonstone to infuse it with energies for divination, feminine magic, and to connect with the goddess, and to connect with the energies of the full moon.

For a quick infusion, hold your weed (or other cannabis product) in your nondominant hand with your moonstone in your dominant hand. Move the moonstone all over and around the weed and say:

> *Send your energies from here to there,*
> *Infuse this [weed, gummy, THC, etc.]*
> *With magic's care.*
> *When it comes to the needed hour,*
> *This [weed, gummy, THC, etc.] contains moonstone's*
> *power.*

For a deeper charge, dedicate a small box, chest, or other type of container where you can charge your cannabis by placing it, along with a moonstone or chips, inside. Add charging with your moonstone to your monthly full moon practices.

NOVEMBER 16
SACRED SMOKE

Sakae naa leaf is used to stimulate creativity and to energize the mind. Combining it with indica strains sparks inspiration. Combining it with a sativa strain energizes the body and mind and is an ideal accompaniment for magical movement.

Introduce yourself to sakae naa leaf by using it on its own several times first, exploring it with all your senses. How does it look? Smell? Feel? Taste? You may either smoke it or make a tealike infusion by soaking the leaves in hot water to drink.

How does it affect you? What do you feel when using it? How long does it take to feel the effects? How long do the effects last?

Evaluate and learn how sakae naa leaf works with your body and mind. Document this information in your Book of Shadows. Once you become familiar with this herb, combine it with cannabis and again explore the effects, being sure to document your results. This herb can be combined with others to create blends.

NOVEMBER 17
KITCHEN WITCHERY

In the morning, combine the following ingredients in a pot of water to simmer throughout the day. Use this on days when you want to boost your communication skills or increase honest communication. Be sure to start your simmer pot early so it has time to simmer and get the energies and magic started around you.

You will need:

- ¼ cup maple syrup
- 9 whole allspice

- 1 tablespoon chamomile (dried or fresh)
- 1 teaspoon marigold petals (dried or fresh)
- 1 teaspoon sacred lotus petals (dried or fresh)
- Pinch of cannabis (dried or fresh)

As you prepare the ingredients and add them to the pot, pour intention into your work. Focus on opening the lines of communication. If there is a specific person or situation you need to address, keep it in mind.

Keep the pot on a low flame on a back burner. Stir the pot nine times clockwise once every hour throughout the day.

Each time you stir the pot, say:

Fire, water, earth, and air,
Fruits from the earth simmer near.
Open truth to be spoken here,
Honest words, nothing to fear.

Add more water as needed to replenish what has evaporated. At the end of the day, pour the remains outside on the ground near a tree or under a bush. Return the plant material to the earth it came from. Add this recipe to your BOS and record your own experience with it.

NOVEMBER 18
EMBRACING THE ELEMENTS

Collect distinct types of precipitation to store in your witch's cupboard. This water can be used to make moon or sun water, and it can be filtered for bong water.

Label your waters with the type of precipitation and the energies within each one. Water collected from a gentle misting drizzle may have calming, even thankful, energies, while melted snow from a damaging blizzard may have more destructive energies. Although lightning is negatively charged, the rain from lightning storms contains powerful positive energy. Keep a running inventory of the waters you have.

NOVEMBER 19
ETHEREAL ESSENCES

Research the different correspondences and uses associated with turmeric and add a supply to your witch's cupboard. Add the information you find to your BOS. Dried turmeric can be smoked, combined with cannabis, or made into a tea. Meet the essence of turmeric in the following meditative practice.

Get into an elevated high and comfortable position with a small container of turmeric, a bottle of oil, or incense lit and placed in front of you.

Close your eyes and take several deep breaths. Allow your mind to settle and focus. When you are ready, pick up the turmeric and hold it about four inches away from your nose. Inhale the scent, breathing deeply. If it's not too overpowering for you, move it closer. Some people have sensitivities, so don't feel you have to move it directly under your nose. Oils are very potent and do not need to be moved as close.

How does this scent make you feel? Is it pleasing? Irritating? Relaxing? Exciting? Powerful? Meditate on the feelings it evokes in you.

Journal about your experience. If you feel the need to clear the scent from your nose, sniff coffee beans or grounds to help neutralize the scent.

NOVEMBER 20
HERBAL INFUSIONS

Combine water and earth together in this bong water herbal infusion to open the lines of communication.

You will need:

- Chamomile (dried)
- Dandelion (dried)

- Jasmine (dried)
- Lavender (dried)

Combine equal amounts of the herbs together to steep. Use this water in your bong or drink it as tea. Add this recipe to your Book of Shadows and record your own experience with it.

NOVEMBER 21
VIBING

Experiment with the following types of frequency-based music to see how they affect you.

- 639 Hz activates the heart chakra to assist in connections and healing relationships.
- 741 Hz activates the throat chakra and helps with communication and expressing the truth.

Use a search engine or music service to find music in these different frequencies to listen to, preferably with headphones. Get high to experience how these frequencies feel to you. Journal about your experience.

NOVEMBER 22
SOULFUL SEARCHING

Get high today to meditate and journal about who your heroes are. Choose a couple or a few to focus on. What do you admire about each of these people? What commonalities do they share? How have your heroes inspired your life?

NOVEMBER 23
RECLAIMING THE SHADOW

Meet your higher self in a deep meditation. Focus on the following questions: What is your worst trait? Where did it come from? What do you gain from using it? How can you change it? Journal about your experience.

NOVEMBER 24
DANK DIVINATION

Osteomancy is divination through bone casting. Sets are available to buy, or you can do an internet search on how to make your own.

You will need:

- 2 black candles

- Lighter

- Casting bones

- Cannabis incense (optional for nonsmokers)

In a dark or dimly lit room, light two black candles and place them about twelve inches in front of you and ten inches apart.

Before you cast your bones, smoke or vape your weed and exhale gently, blowing the smoke over them and in between the two candles while opening your mind to receiving a message from Spirit. Cast the bones into the area between you and the candles. If you do not smoke, consume your cannabis in your normal manner and wave the smoke from a cannabis incense stick over the bones.

Record your experience in your Book of Shadows along with any information you obtain through research on osteomancy.

NOVEMBER 25
MEDITATION MOJO

Get into a comfortable position and slip into a meditative high. Contemplate what you are thankful for but focus on yourself and your own traits, abilities, achievements, etc. What have you done for which you are thankful? Journal after your meditation.

NOVEMBER 26
HERBAL BLENDS

Use this blend on its own for a boost or to accompany your communication-themed spellwork.

You will need:

- Blue lotus (dried)
- Chamomile (dried)
- Dandelion leaves (dried)
- Lavender (dried)
- Motherwort (dried)
- Sacred lotus (dried)
- Tulsi (dried)

Combine equal parts of all the herbs. Grind them together and then blend with your weed in a one-to-one ratio whenever you need to open the lines of communication.

As you combine and grind your herbs together, focus on skillful communication and getting your point across while also listening to what is said. This will infuse the blend with your intention and energy.

Add this recipe, how it feels, and your results to your Book of Shadows. If you desire, adjust ratios for flavor.

NOVEMBER 27
FIND YOUR WILD

Connect to the night sky with a good high. You do not have to see the stars with your physical eyes if you picture them in your mind's eye. A galaxy map can show you where you are in relation to constellations and the moon to help you get your bearings and give you images to visualize.

Stand outside in the dark with your face to the sky. Either stare into space, taking in everything you can see—the stars, the moon, even satellites and airplanes cutting across the sky—or if it is too cloudy or your view is disrupted by light pollution, picture them in your mind. The energies of air and celestial bodies are all around you. How do these energies feel to you? How do you differentiate them from one another? How can you best utilize them? Add this information to your BOS.

This exercise will be done monthly throughout the year because as the night sky changes, the energies you feel will also change.

NOVEMBER 28
MAGICAL MUSICAL MOVEMENT

Start a playlist of songs with a theme of releasing and letting go. When you are stressed out, what music helps you release it? This playlist can be used during prep and spellwork or other workings. Be sure to check out frequency-based music.

Try out your playlist by getting high and choosing a few songs to move to in whatever type of movement you prefer, even if it is only rocking back and forth.

Try listening to your playlist motionless with your eyes closed or with a blindfold to block out other distractions. Use headphones if possible. Does it create the energy and environment you desire?

NOVEMBER 29
INTRIGUING INCANTATIONS

To open communication, say:

When the lines of communication are confused and blocked,
And the hearts involved are closed and locked,
Openness and understanding are needed to heal,
I call upon magic to seal the deal.

Use this chant on its own or in addition to other spellwork.

NOVEMBER 30
SOULFUL SEARCHING

This month you focused on both internal and external communication. What did you find helpful? What areas of communication do you still struggle with? How can improved communication skills impact your spirituality or practice?

December

As we move into winter, the time for rest and inner workings is at hand. This month you will focus on sleep and all the magic it brings with it.

December Supply List
December 2

> 6 × 6-inch square piece of blue material
>
> Amethyst
>
> Moonstone
>
> Jet
>
> Apple seeds
>
> Essential oil, dried herb, or resin: jasmine, lavender, rose, valerian, violet
>
> Dried: sacred lotus petals, blue vervain

6 inches of blue ribbon

Cannabis incense (optional for nonsmokers)

December 5

Glass jar with lid or corked vial

Dried: bergamot, chamomile, dandelion, jasmine, lavender, passionflower, valerian

Amethyst chips

Cannabis ash

Black sealing wax

Blue sealing wax

December 8

Your water charger

Carnelian

Clear quartz

Peppermint

December 12

Calea zacatechichi

Mugwort

December 14

Cannabis incense (optional for nonsmokers)

December 16

Sacred lotus flower

December 17

Dried or fresh: lavender buds, sacred lotus petals,
jasmine buds, rose petals, vervain, cannabis

December 18

Glass jar with lid or corked vial

Onyx chips

Dried: rosemary, rue, St. John's wort, thyme, mullein

Black sealing wax

Blue sealing wax

White sealing wax

Enough black twine to wrap around the top of
your jar and tie on a charm

White full moon charm

December 19

Peppermint

December 20

Your water charger

Chamomile

Jasmine

Lavender

Passionflower

Valerian

Blue vervain

Moonstone

December 22

Glass jar or corked vial

Dried: bergamot, blue vervain, clover, dandelion, lavender, marigold, mugwort, violet, yarrow

Clear quartz chips

Sodalite chips

Black sealing wax

Blue sealing wax

Enough gray twine to wrap around the top of your jar and tie on a charm

Moon charm

December 26

> Dried: blue lotus, blue vervain, catnip, chamomile, hops, jasmine, lavender, lemon balm, mugwort, passionflower, sacred lotus

December 31

> Black spell-size candle
>
> Purple spell-size candle
>
> Lighter
>
> Dragon's blood incense
>
> Dried: mugwort, blue vervain, wormwood

DECEMBER 1
LIT LITERATURE

Cannabis can be a great tool to help us remember and access our past lives. Learn more about past lives in your reading this month. No matter where you shop for books, use the keywords "past lives" in your search to find titles of interest.

DECEMBER 2
TEMPTING TALISMAN

This talisman encourages restorative sleep to help you feel recharged and restored. Give your body an energetic break and allow it time to ground and recover. Try to use a mix of oils and dried ingredients if available to you. Use a pinch of dried ingredients and a drop or two of oils.

You will need:

- 6 × 6-inch square of blue material
- Amethyst
- Moonstone
- Jet
- Apple seeds
- Jasmine (essential oil, dried herb, or resin)
- Lavender (essential oil, dried herb, or resin)
- Rose (essential oil, dried herb, or resin)
- Valerian (essential oil, dried herb, or resin)
- Violet (essential oil, dried herb, or resin)
- Sacred lotus petals (dried)
- Blue vervain (dried)

- 6 inches of blue ribbon
- Cannabis incense (optional for nonsmokers)

Smoke your weed (or use another consumption method) while you assemble your ingredients and create this talisman. If you have room to work at your altar, do so, or create another sacred space where you have room and are comfortable.

Lay the blue square on your altar or other stable location. Begin with the largest ingredients you are working with, most likely your stones in this instance. Add them to the center of the material.

Next, add any smaller dried herbs or flowers. Top these off with one drop of any essential oils you use. Drip them onto a dried herb or flower so they soak into those instead of the material.

When you are done filling it, bunch the material up into a pouch and wrap the ribbon around the neck three times before knotting it off.

Use this chant to help guide your intentions and work:

Draw to me the energies of restorative sleep,
Close my mind to worries.
Help my body, mind, and soul
To rest and recharge in peace.

Take a hit and release your intention and exhale your smoke all over the pouch. (You may also use the smoke from cannabis incense along with your own breath.)

Store your talisman on your altar or in another magical, safe space. When you need its power, place it under your pillow and repeat the above chant to activate its magic.

DECEMBER 3
SOULFUL SEARCHING

Get high for this meditative journaling session. This month's astrological house represents your service and sacrifice. Journal about how service and sacrifice play a role in your current practice. What aspects are you proud of? What improvements do you want to make?

DECEMBER 4
ASTROLOGICAL HOUSES

Research the meaning of the astrological twelfth house and explore the role it plays in your life within your own chart. The twelfth house represents service and sacrifice. Record the information you learn and how it relates to your sign and yourself in your Book of Shadows or a journal.

DECEMBER 5
DELIGHTFUL DABBLING

Tap into magic on the nights you want a restful, dream-free sleep. When too many thoughts are running through your mind or you feel anxious or overwhelmed, encourage peaceful sleep with this spell jar.

You will need:

- Glass jar with lid or corked vial
- Bergamot (dried)
- Chamomile (dried)
- Dandelion (dried)
- Jasmine (dried)
- Lavender (dried)
- Passionflower (dried)
- Valerian (dried)
- Amethyst chips
- Cannabis ash
- Black sealing wax
- Blue sealing wax

Smoke your weed (or use another consumption method, allowing time for edibles to take effect).

Place each ingredient into your chosen jar (or mix them in a bowl and then transfer them to your jar), focusing on each one's energy along with your intention. Visualize a protective bubble being created around you as you build and bless your jar.

As you work with each ingredient, say:

I call upon the energies of [ingredient name],
Store your magic here for me,
'Til needed later,
Blessed be.

Take a hit (or deep, centered, intention-filled breath if you do not smoke or vape) and use your exhalation to gently blow your hopes and objectives into your jar.

Close the top of the jar and cover it with the melted sealing wax, first black and then blue, allowing both colors to show. When finished, activate your jar by saying:

Calm my mind,
Bring me peace,
Give me a night,
Of calming sleep.

Place it next to your bed on nights you need a calming, peaceful sleep.

DECEMBER 6
CERRIDWEN'S CAULDRON

Research the distinct types of dream work. Dream analysis is one aspect, while lucid dreaming is another. Each of these categories is quite different and can contribute directly to your practice. Broaden your knowledge of what the brain is capable of while you sleep.

DECEMBER 7
LIFTED PERSPECTIVE

During the dark half of the year, it's easy for the darkness to sometimes feel depressing or even overwhelming. Always remember, you are your own pharmacy when it comes to endorphin production. You can manufacture and manifest them simply by enjoying yourself. So do that. Give yourself a good, happy high and do something that makes you laugh. Watch a comedy show or listen to a funny podcast or audiobook. Manifest that happy high into positive energy and chill in the afterglow. Magic can be found everywhere. Lift your own perspective when needed.

DECEMBER 8
DELIGHTFUL DABBLING

Using your water charger, combine water and earth together in this bong water herbal infusion for mental energy.

You will need:

- Your water charger
- Carnelian
- Clear quartz
- Peppermint

You may either add the peppermint to the water to steep or place it with the carnelian and quartz separate from your water but in close proximity. Use this water in your bong with a sativa blend (or drink it) for a mental energy brain boost.

DECEMBER 9
FIND YOUR WILD

Discover the history of the land where you live. What animal life is native to your area? What is endangered? What species are invasive? What steps can you take to help conserve or restore habitat? In what ways can you connect with this animal life?

DECEMBER 10
EMBRACING THE ELEMENTS

The darkest nights of the year are at hand, and while today we have electricity to battle against this darkness, our ancestors relied on the light and warmth of fire to endure the long, cold, difficult nights. Fire not only kept them alive; it also gave them hope to survive through the winter. We do not have the same relationship with fire as our forebears. Meditate on what fire means for you today. What role does it play in your life? In your practice? What emotions does fire evoke in you?

DECEMBER 11
GROWING WITH THE GREEN MAN

Take your high outside today, in the later evening if possible. The earth has gone still. Much of nature is silent and at rest. Try to close out any manufactured noises around you. Eliminate them from your focus. Try to recognize and detect the lower and slower vibrations of winter around you.

DECEMBER 12
SUPERNATURAL SENSES

While lucid dream work can be quite difficult, intention mixed with consumption of a dream blend before bed can aid in triggering the subconscious to awaken in the dream world.

You will need:

- *Calea zacatechichi*
- Mugwort

Blend together equal amounts of *Calea zacatechichi* and mugwort and then combine with your cannabis in a fifty-fifty mix and smoke or drink as a tea before bed.

Set your intention to be aware and lucid during your dreaming state. Program a digital reminder with your alarm or put a sign where you will see it immediately upon waking, reminding you to attempt dream recall right away. The sooner you attempt dream recall, the more chance of success.

DECEMBER 13
RECLAIMING THE SHADOW

Meet your higher self in a deep meditation and focus on the following questions: How do I deal with rejection? Why do

I react this way? What better options can I try in the future? Journal about your experience.

DECEMBER 14
DANK DIVINATION

Smoke or vape your weed and blow the smoke over your tarot or oracle cards as you shuffle them, focusing on the past year. (You may consume your cannabis in a different form and use the smoke from cannabis incense.) Lay out eight cards in a line to read as follows:

Card 1. What I learned.

Card 2. What I gained.

Card 3. What I lost.

Card 4. What I overcame.

Card 5. What I accomplished.

Card 6. What I kept hidden.

Card 7. What I revealed.

Card 8. Where I am now.

Document your drawn cards and their meanings in your journal. Explore your reading in meditation.

DECEMBER 15
SOULFUL SEARCHING

Write a letter to your younger self at a time when you didn't feel supported by those around you. Choose whichever age resonates the most with you. Tell yourself what you wish you could have heard back then that you didn't hear. Be your own best advocate. Tell yourself how you overcame obstacles and dealt with issues that stood in your way. Remind yourself you survived.

DECEMBER 16
SACRED SMOKE

Sacred lotus flower is both a sleep aid and a mood enhancer. It delivers waves of calmness over the user.

Introduce yourself to sacred lotus flower by using it on its own several times first, exploring it with all your senses. How does it look? Smell? Feel? Taste? You may either smoke it or make a tealike infusion by soaking the leaves in hot water to drink.

How does it affect you? What do you feel when using it? How long does it take to feel the effects? How long do the effects last?

Evaluate and learn how sacred lotus flower works with your body and mind. Document this information in your Book of Shadows.

Once you become familiar with this herb, combine it with cannabis and again explore the effects, being sure to document your results. This herb can be combined with others to create blends.

DECEMBER 17
KITCHEN WITCHERY

In the late afternoon, combine the following ingredients in a pot of water to simmer for several hours before bed. This will create an aura to support restful sleep.

You will need:

- ¼ cup lavender buds (dried or fresh)
- 1 tablespoon sacred lotus petals (dried or fresh)
- 1 tablespoon jasmine buds (dried or fresh)
- ¼ cup rose petals (dried or fresh)
- 1 tablespoon vervain (dried or fresh)
- Pinch of cannabis (dried or fresh)

As you prepare the ingredients and add them to the pot, pour intention into your work. Focus on achieving peaceful, restful sleep.

Keep the pot on a low flame on a back burner. Stir the pot nine times clockwise once every hour throughout the time you have it simmering.

Each time you stir the pot, say:

Fire, water, earth, and air,
Fruits from the earth simmer here.
Listen to the words I say,
Bring restful sleep to end my day.

Add more water as needed to replenish what has evaporated. At the end of the day, pour the remains outside on the ground near a tree or under a bush. Return the plant material to the earth it came from.

You can also use lavender, lotus, jasmine, rose, and vervain essential oils in a diffuser while you sleep. Recite the chant as you add the drops to your diffuser, where the oils will do their own kind of "simmer." Add this recipe to your BOS and record your own experience with it.

DECEMBER 18
DELIGHTFUL DABBLING

Create this spell jar to keep nightmares and other bad dreams at bay while you sleep.

You will need:

- Glass jar with lid or corked vial
- Onyx chips
- Rosemary (dried)
- Rue (dried)
- St. John's wort (dried)
- Thyme (dried)
- Mullein (dried)
- Black sealing wax
- Blue sealing wax
- White sealing wax
- Enough black twine to wrap around the top of your jar and tie on a charm
- White full moon charm

Smoke your weed (or use another consumption method, allowing time for edibles to take effect).

Place each ingredient into your chosen jar (or mix them in a bowl and then transfer them to your jar), focusing on each one's energy along with your intention. Visualize a protective bubble being created around you as you build and bless your jar.

As you work with each ingredient, say:

> I call upon the energies of [ingredient name],
> Protect me in my sleep.

Take a hit (or deep, centered, intention-filled breath if you do not smoke or vape) and use your exhalation to gently blow your hopes and objectives into your jar.

Close the top of the jar and cover it with the melted sealing wax, first the black, then the blue, and finally the white, allowing all colors to show. Wrap the string around the jar top and attach the charm. When finished, say:

> Keep my dreams safe and happy,
> Let them entertain and educate me.
> Keep me safe through the night,
> Nightmare free through morning light.

Place it next to, or under, your bed to create a safe, comfy bubble of protection around you.

DECEMBER 19
ETHEREAL ESSENCES

Research the different correspondences and uses associated with peppermint and add a supply to your witch's cupboard. Add the information you find to your BOS. Dried peppermint can be smoked, combined with cannabis, or made into a tea. Meet the essence of peppermint in the following meditative practice.

Get into an elevated high and comfortable position with a small container of dried peppermint, a bottle of oil, or incense lit and placed in front of you.

Close your eyes and take several deep breaths. Allow your mind to settle and focus. When you are ready, pick up the peppermint and hold it about eight inches away from your nose. Inhale the scent, breathing deeply. If it's not too overpowering for you, move it closer. Some people have sensitivities, so don't feel you have to move it directly under your nose. Oils are very potent and do not need to be moved as close.

How does this scent make you feel? Is it pleasing? Irritating? Relaxing? Exciting? Powerful? Meditate on the feelings it evokes in you.

Journal about your experience. If you feel the need to clear the scent from your nose, sniff coffee beans or grounds to help neutralize the scent.

DECEMBER 20
HERBAL INFUSIONS

Using your water charger, combine water and earth together in this bong water herbal infusion for peaceful sleep.

You will need:

- Your water charger
- Chamomile
- Jasmine
- Lavender
- Passionflower
- Valerian
- Blue vervain
- Moonstone

You may either add the herbs to steep or place them with the moonstone separate from your water but in close proximity. Use this water in your bong with an indica blend or drink it as tea before bed.

DECEMBER 21
VIBING

Binaural beats use different tones and different frequencies in each ear. Binaural beats can be found in different frequencies for different uses. Use a search engine or music service to find binaural beats for sleep to listen to, preferably with headphones. Get high to experience how these binaural beats affect you. Journal about your experience.

DECEMBER 22
DELIGHTFUL DABBLING

Create this spell jar to aid you in lucid dreams and other psychic dream work.

You will need:

- Glass jar or corked vial
- Bergamot (dried)
- Blue vervain (dried)
- Clover (dried)
- Dandelion (dried)
- Lavender (dried)

- Marigold (dried)

- Mugwort (dried)

- Violet (dried)

- Yarrow (dried)

- Clear quartz chips

- Sodalite chips

- Black sealing wax

- Blue sealing wax

- Enough gray twine to wrap around the top of your jar and tie on a charm

- Moon charm

Smoke your weed (or use another consumption method, allowing time for edibles to take effect).

Place each ingredient into your chosen jar (or mix them in a bowl and then transfer them to your jar), focusing on each one's energy along with your intention.

As you work with each ingredient, say:

I call upon the energies of [ingredient name],
Bring magic to my dreams.

Take a hit (or deep, centered, intention-filled breath if you do not smoke or vape) and use your exhalation to gently blow your hopes and objectives into your jar.

Close the top of the jar and cover it with melted sealing wax, first the black and then the blue, allowing both colors to show. Wrap the string around the jar top and attach the charm.

Activate your jar by saying:

> *Create around me*
> *A liminal space*
> *In which I enter my dreams.*
> *Send me messages to understand*
> *What the universe deems.*

Place the jar next to or under your bed.

DECEMBER 23
RECLAIMING THE SHADOW

Get into a deep meditative state and connect with your higher self. What boundaries do you have a challenging time respecting for both others and you? Ask yourself why and follow your answers back until you find the root of this behavior. Why are these boundaries difficult to respect? How can you change this in the future? Journal about your experience.

DECEMBER 24
DANK DIVINATION

Load up your pipe and practice with your pendulum. If you wish, add mugwort or a divination blend of smokable herbs to your weed. You may also consume your weed in another method and drink mugwort tea. If you do not have a pendulum, you can easily make one with something heavy like a ring or key attached to the end of a string.

Use your pendulum for a baseline before you smoke your pipe. What differences do you notice after you employ your weed? Journal about the results you receive.

Research using pendulums and document what you find in your BOS. If you are more practiced with pendulums, do you have a favorite one or pendulums with special meanings or stones? Describe your overall experience with pendulums and inventory any you possess in your BOS.

DECEMBER 25
MEDITATION MOJO

No matter what your religious views are, the secular portrayal of Christmas idolizes a jolly immortal elf, and that is its own special kind of magic. The world over, billions of people believe in the concept of a "Santa Claus," though the name and details vary.

Today, get high and meditate on your version of Santa Claus. What does he look like? How does he sound? And yes, how does he smell? Imagine your own private meeting with Santa. Where do you go and what do you do? What do you talk about? Happy Santa Day!

DECEMBER 26
HERBAL BLENDS

This blend is to promote a good night's sleep.

You will need:

- Blue lotus (dried)
- Blue vervain (dried)
- Catnip (dried)
- Chamomile (dried)
- Hops (dried)
- Jasmine (dried)
- Lavender (dried)
- Lemon balm (dried)
- Mugwort (dried)

- Passionflower (dried)
- Sacred lotus (dried)

Combine equal amounts of each herb. Grind them together and blend with your weed in a one-to-one ratio before settling down for a good night's sleep. As you combine and grind your herbs together, focus on restful sleep to further infuse the blend with your intention and energy.

Add this recipe, how it feels, and your results to your Book of Shadows. If you desire, adjust ratios for flavor.

DECEMBER 27
FIND YOUR WILD

Connect to the night sky with a good high. You do not have to see the stars with your physical eyes if you picture them in your mind's eye. A galaxy map can show you where you are in relation to constellations and the moon to help you get your bearings and give you images to visualize.

Stand outside in the dark with your face to the sky. Either stare into space, taking in everything you can see—the stars, the moon, even satellites and airplanes cutting across the sky—or if it is too cloudy or your view is disrupted by light pollution, picture them in your mind. The energies of air and celestial bodies are all around you. How do these energies feel to you? How do you differentiate them from one another? How can you best utilize them? Add this information to your BOS.

This exercise will be done monthly throughout the year because as the night sky changes, the energies you feel will also change.

DECEMBER 28
MAGICAL MUSICAL MOVEMENT

Start a playlist of songs with a theme of rest. What songs let you restfully relax and unwind? This playlist can be used during prep, spellwork, other workings, before sleep, or just when you need a moment to rest in order to recharge. Be sure to check out frequency-based music.

Try out your playlist by getting high and choosing a few songs to move to in whatever type of movement you prefer, even if it is only rocking back and forth.

Try listening to your playlist motionless with your eyes closed or with a blindfold to block out other distractions. Use headphones if possible. Does it create the energy and environment you desire?

DECEMBER 29
INTRIGUING INCANTATIONS

For a good night's sleep, say:

> *Now I lay me down to rest,*
> *It's what I need to be my best.*
> *Heal my body, mind, and soul,*
> *So I can awake refreshed and whole.*

Use this chant before bed either alone or in addition to other spellwork.

DECEMBER 30
SOULFUL SEARCHING

How do you feel after a month of paying attention to your sleep and focusing on dream work? What changes have you felt with the internalization of your energy as you focus on restorative rest? How has your dream work aided your practice and spirituality?

DECEMBER 31
DELIGHTFUL DABBLING

This working is to guide you in releasing what you wish to before the year ends at midnight.

You will need:

- Black spell-size candle
- Purple spell-size candle
- Lighter
- Dragon's blood incense
- Mugwort (dried)
- Blue vervain (dried)
- Wormwood (dried)

Light your candles and the incense. Then, mix a blend of equal amounts of mugwort, blue vervain, and wormwood and grind together. Combine in a one-to-one ratio with your weed or prepare and drink as tea.

If smoking, load your bong and smoke a full bowl (or take a hit if you have a lower tolerance level). Focus on events that occurred over the past year. Begin with any negative events or situations. You do not need to go into deep details of these negativities, but instead, gather all of this heartache together in one collective ball in your chest.

Take another hit or smoke another bowlful. As you inhale, visualize the smoke in your lungs grabbing ahold of this collection. Remove the bowl from your bong and gently blow the smoke back through the mouthpiece into the bong. Your smoke cleanses you of these negative energies and pours them back into your bong water.

Set the bong aside until a little before midnight and then pour the water onto the ground. Clean your bong before using it again.

Chapter 3
LUNAR RITUALS

In this section, you will find moon workings in a set format to help you build your own moon rituals practice. Creating a ritual format helps you transition from mundane to spiritual work. It trains your mind to shift to a higher consciousness or to recognize a connection to deity is coming. This is a basic starting point from which to build and customize your rituals. Keeping your moon rituals slightly different from other rituals helps to set them apart; this is why I choose to work with bong water, crystals, and blends for lunar rituals.

Included are suggestions for crystals to charge your weed or bong (moon) water with, herbs for bong water infusion, and a blend to use for smoking or to make an herbal infusion for nonsmokers. You will add your cannabis flower to the blend to smoke, add THC to your infusion, or take an edible while you drink your infusion.

What you use in your blend or your bong water can be interchanged to your own preferences using their given correspondences. When preparing and working with your supplies, always be mindful of your intentions and what intention each ingredient fulfills. Crystals may be used to charge both your weed and your bong water.

Prepare your blends three days ahead of time. This gives them time to be charged by the recommended crystal while working under the effects of the same moon phase. Find yourself a special container to store your weed in while it is charging. It should have some type of cover or lid to keep dust and other debris out.

For best results, when possible, perform your ritual outside under the new or full moon and add music, incense, or both if you desire.

January New Moon

Intention: Use the dark of the moon to clear out what you don't need to make way for new beginnings. Tie up endings and take time for rest. Prepare to recharge yourself as the moon begins to grow full.

Bong water: Wormwood to remove obstacles standing in your way of letting go.

Crystal: Obsidian to absorb negativities.

Blend: White sage for connection to your higher self. Mugwort for purification and the creativity to think outside of the box, when necessary, to solve problems. Skullcap for mental focus and clarity and to help you "see" what may still be hidden in the dark.

Process: Use a space where you can sit comfortably and meditate. Set up this space with your prepared supplies: bong with wormwood-infused water (if using), herbal blend, smoking or tea supplies, and the following:

- Spell-size black candle
- Black candleholder
- Lighter
- Small piece of paper and a safe way to burn it (Step outside if you wish or to another location.)
- Writing instrument

When you are prepared and in place, light the candle. Then, ritualistically consume your blend and cannabis in a meaningful and mindful manner. Position yourself for meditation and allow the magic time to take place. (If you are using edibles, take them ahead of time to give them a chance to activate in your system.)

Meditate on any loose ends you have, emotional baggage, and mental trash to clean out. Whether they be big or small, think about the things that nag at your mind, even in the hidden recesses. Bring these things to the surface now.

Write down brief keywords of the ends you need tied up, those things you need to dispel, and the trash you want to dispose of on your piece of paper. Take the paper outside, safely burn it, and say:

> *Here I stand in the dark of night,*
> *Take these things from my life.*

Allow the ash to blow away.

January Full Moon (Wolf)

Intention: Send energies for success to your current ventures or projects.

Bong water: Chamomile and lemon balm to help manifest your success.

Crystal: Green aventurine for success.

Blend: Wormwood and mugwort to spark your creativity. Lemon balm to increase your success.

Process: Use a space where you can sit comfortably to work. Set up this space with your prepared supplies: bong with infused water (if using), herbal blend, smoking or tea supplies, and the following:

- Spell-size green candle
- Candleholder
- Lighter
- Small piece of paper and a safe way to burn it
  (Step outside if you wish or to another location.)
- Writing instrument

When you are prepared and in place, ritualistically consume your blend and cannabis in a meaningful and mindful manner. Position yourself for meditation and allow the magic time to take place. (If you are using edibles, take them ahead of time to give them a chance to activate in your system.) Light your candle.

Meditate on your current ventures or projects. Visualize them as already successfully completed. Your hard work paid off. Your goals are accomplished. Enjoy the feelings of achievement.

Write down keywords that represent your success. Tell the universe that this is what you want. You will not settle for less.

Take a hit and blow your intention for success across the paper. (If you are a nonsmoker, take a mindful breath, and as you exhale, blow your intention across the paper.) Roll it into a thin scroll to light from your candle and drop it into a fire-safe container. (Or you may burn it outside.) As it burns, say:

Moon above, full and bright,
Undeniable success I seek tonight.
I have the power; I have the fight.
This is my will; this is my might.

Allow the ashes to blow away.

February New Moon

Intention: This dark moon is a suitable time for introspection and dealing with the most difficult challenges in your emotional healing. Your higher self will help you walk through these challenges if you ask.

Bong water: Mullein for healing.

Crystals: Clear quartz for its healing and amplifying qualities and to help make the hidden clear. Rose quartz for nurturing the self.

Blend: Blue vervain to assist in connecting to your higher self for shadow work. Blue lotus flower to open your mind and for spiritual connection. Mugwort for psychic connection and visions of what work needs to be done.

Process: Use a space where you can sit comfortably and meditate. Set up this space with your prepared supplies: bong with mullein-infused water (if using), herbal blend, smoking or tea supplies.

When you are prepared and in place, ritualistically consume your blend and cannabis in a meaningful and mindful manner. Position yourself for meditation and allow the magic time to take place. (If you are using edibles, take them ahead of time to give them a chance to activate in your system.)

Allow yourself to go into a deep, trancelike meditation. Your higher self or power has a message for you this dark moon about where you need to focus your healing. Don't fight it. Let it lead you where you need to go.

February Full Moon (Snow, Storm, Hunger)

Intention: To discover positive solutions to emotional healing through redirection and thinking outside of the box. Let your higher self lead you to new possibilities.

Bong water: Rose petals for nourishing the self.

Crystal: Carnelian for creative solutions.

Blend: Wormwood and mugwort for creativity. Hyssop to remove stagnation from the soul. Motherwort for emotional support.

Process: Use a space where you can sit comfortably and meditate. Set up this space with your prepared supplies: bong with rose petal–infused water (if using), herbal blend, and your smoking or tea supplies.

When you are prepared and in place, ritualistically consume your blend and cannabis in a meaningful and mindful manner. Say:

> *Moon above, full and bright,*
> *Bring my darkness into the light.*
> *Help me to see, guide my sight,*
> *So I can heal; set my heart right.*

Position yourself for meditation and allow the magic time to take place. (If you are using edibles, take them ahead of time to give them a chance to activate in your system.)

Open yourself to connection with your higher self. If you have a specific issue you are dealing with, seek insight and look at it from your higher point of view instead of your mundane one. If you do not have a specific issue you want to address, allow your higher self to choose one for you. Listen to what this self has to say; it has sage advice to help you on your healing journey. What solutions does it offer? Let it guide you to what your next steps should be.

March New Moon

Intention: Remove stagnant or blocked energies that interrupt the flow of positive energies, or what we refer to as "luck."

Bong water: Clove for purification.

Crystals: Obsidian to absorb negativity and quartz for cleansing.

Blend: White sage to remove negative energies. Hyssop for protection from negative influences and to remove negative energy.

Process: Use a space where you can sit comfortably and work. Set up this space with your prepared supplies: bong with infused water (if using), herbal blend, and smoking or tea supplies. You will also need your obsidian and quartz.

When you are prepared and in place, ritualistically consume your blend and cannabis in a meaningful and mindful manner. Position yourself for meditation and allow the magic time to take place. (If you are using edibles, take them ahead of time to give them a chance to activate in your system.)

Hold the quartz in your dominant hand and the obsidian in the other. Visualize fresh, clean, vibrant energy being sucked into the quartz from the area around you. Imagine the quartz taking in a rainbow of colored energies. Watch these energies travel from the quartz into your hand, your wrist, your arm, up into your shoulder where they then dive down into your chest, your legs, back up through your torso, your neck, your head, back into the other shoulder, down the arm, into your hand, and finally into the obsidian. As they travel, they push along the path in front of them any dingy, cloudy, negative energies they encounter. Let these energies scrub you clean and refreshed. When you are finished, bury the obsidian in the ground to let it cleanse.

March Full Moon (Worm, Plow, Moon of Winds)

Intention: To magically combine luck with hope to equal success.

Bong water: Chopped strawberries for luck. (These may be fresh or dehydrated, just ensure the pieces are small enough you will still be able to clean them out of your bong after they rehydrate and expand in your water.)

Crystals: Green aventurine for success and quartz for hope and amplifying power.

Blend: Dried strawberries crushed into small chunks for luck. Catnip, rose, and lavender for luck.

Process: Use a space where you can sit comfortably and meditate. Set up this space with your prepared supplies: bong with infused water (if using) herbal blend, smoking or tea supplies, and the following:

- Spell-size green candle
- Lighter
- Small piece of paper and a safe way to burn it (Step outside if you wish or to another location.)
- Writing instrument

When you are prepared and in place, ritualistically consume your blend and cannabis in a meaningful and mindful manner. Light the green candle.

Position yourself for meditation, holding on to your paper, and allow the magic time to take place. (If you are using edibles, take them ahead of time to give them a chance to activate in your system.)

Center yourself and your thoughts. What is it you hope for? What success are you looking for? How can luck assist you? Write your hope on the paper and roll it into a thin, tight scroll.

Focus on the luck you want to attract and say:

> *By the moon above and the earth below,*
> *I call these powers now to show:*
> *Take my wish into the universe,*
> *Energies here to disperse.*
> *Transform them, bend them to my will,*
> *Return to me success, my hope fulfilled.*

Light the scroll from your candle and drop it into a fire-safe container to burn, releasing your wishes into the ether.

April New Moon

Intention: Use the dark of the moon to weed out your unloving actions and habits toward yourself and others.

Bong water: Rose petals for nourishing your soul and inner strength.

Incense (Optional): Gardenia for emotional support.

Crystals: Amethyst for spiritual work and obsidian to absorb negative energy.

Blend: White sage to increase your self-awareness and aid in connecting to your higher self or power. Hyssop for expelling negative and stagnant energies.

Process: Use a space where you can sit comfortably and meditate. Set up this space with your prepared supplies: bong with infused water (if using), incense, herbal blend, and smoking or tea supplies.

When you are prepared and in place, ritualistically consume your blend and cannabis in a meaningful and mindful manner. Position yourself for meditation and allow the magic time to take place. (If you are using edibles, take them ahead of time to give them a chance to activate in your system.)

Shift into your higher self where you can objectively, yet gently, evaluate the actions and habits you use when dealing with yourself and others. Allow your higher self to point out any unwanted weeds in your personality. These actions, these habits—you no longer need them. Visualize your higher self picking these weeds right out of your very soul and flinging them away. After your meditation, give yourself strength and support to rid yourself of these traits in the mundane world.

April Full Moon (Pink, Seed)

Intention: This full moon, honor and increase all forms of love in your family and home life.

Bong water: Chamomile to bring peaceful calm into your home.

Crystals: Amethyst for spiritual work. Quartz for a cleansing amplifier.

Blend: Motherwort for nurturing and protective love. Rose petals to enhance, draw, and increase feelings of love.

Process: Use a space where you can sit comfortably and meditate. Set up this space with your prepared supplies: bong with infused water (if using) herbal blend, and smoking or tea supplies.

When you are prepared and in place, ritualistically consume your blend and cannabis in a meaningful and mindful manner. Say:

> *Under this moon, full and bright,*
> *Fill my home with love tonight.*
> *Open minds and open hearts,*
> *Bring love to my life with this rite.*

Position yourself for meditation and allow the magic time to take place. (If you are using edibles, take them ahead of time to give them a chance to activate in your system.)

Meditate on and appreciate the love you currently have in your life. Give thanks for the love you have experienced. Open yourself and your heart to both give and receive love willingly in the future.

May New Moon

Intention: Bring or increase romance (enchantment, charm) and passion (ardor, enthusiasm, zest) in your life. This refers to a variety of emotions including those of a sexual nature.

Bong water: Blue lotus to open your mind.

Crystals: Two rose quartzes for romance.

Blend: Hops, jasmine, damiana and hibiscus for their ability to draw passion into your life.

Process: Use a space where you can sit comfortably and work. Set up this space with your prepared supplies: bong with infused water (if using), herbal blend, smoking or tea supplies, and two rose quartz crystals.

When you are prepared and in place, ritualistically consume your blend and cannabis in a meaningful and mindful manner. Position yourself for meditation and allow the magic time to take place. (If you are using edibles, take them ahead of time to give them a chance to activate in your system.)

Hold a rose quartz in each of your hands with your palms facing upward. Close your eyes and take several deep breaths, relaxing more with each breath. Symbolically visualize what you believe energies of romance and passion may look like. You might see ribbons or waves of pink and red colors floating around you. You may see these energies symbolized by acts of love. You may seem them as happy memories from your past. Whatever works for you, use it. Collect these energies by pulling them into your crystals. Draw them in and store them. Charge the rose quartz with these energies.

Place these crystals in prominent places in your home—one near your bed and the other in a location you feel it will best serve.

May Full Moon (Flower, Hare)

Intention: Mentally plant your seeds for your goals to grow.

Bong water: White sage to help slip into your higher consciousness and increase your self-awareness.

Crystal: Green aventurine to encourage prosperity.

Blend: Skullcap to encourage calmness for meditation and mental focus. Hops to represent fertility, growth, and abundance.

Process: Use a space where you can sit comfortably and meditate. Set up this space with your prepared supplies: bong with infused water (if using), herbal blend, smoking or tea supplies, and the following:

- Small piece of paper
- Writing instrument
- Place in which to bury the paper after ritual

When you are prepared and in place, ritualistically consume your blend and cannabis in a meaningful and mindful manner. Position yourself for meditation and allow the magic time to take place. (If you are using edibles, take them ahead of time to give them a chance to activate in your system.)

Meditate on your goals: What "seeds" do you need to plant in your life? What do you need to grow?

After your meditation, write down a description of your seeds on the paper. As you fold the paper, say:

> *Moon above round and full,*
> *I plant these seeds so they will grow.*
> *These things I speak in the dark of night,*
> *I will work to bring into my life.*

Plant the paper in the ground. If you have a garden plot, plant it there.

June New Moon

Intention: Remove inner obstacles to peace.

Bong water: Hibiscus for overcoming obstacles.

Crystals: Obsidian for neutralizing negativity. Quartz to amplify your power.

Blend: Hyssop to expel obstacles and stagnant energies. Clove for mental focus. Motherwort to support emotional heart burdens and bring peace. Blue lotus flower to open your mind to what you need to see.

Process: Use a space where you can sit comfortably and meditate. Set up this space with your prepared supplies: bong with infused water (if using), herbal blend, smoking or tea supplies, and the following:

- Black candle
- Lighter

When you are prepared and in place, light your candle, then ritualistically consume your blend and cannabis in a meaningful and mindful manner. Position yourself for meditation and allow the magic time to take place. (If you are using edibles, take them ahead of time to give them a chance to activate in your system.)

Connect with your higher power or higher self. Ask for guidance in recognizing the things that keep you from being at peace. Look at these things now objectively. How can you remove these obstacles on your pathway to peace? If you can't remove the obstacle, how can you go around it? The only actions you can control are your own. Peace may be in reach, but obtainable only through a path you did not previously see. Let your higher self guide you on a path to peace and show you how to overcome or circumvent obstacles in the way.

When you are ready, take a hit of your weed. As you inhale, focus on the smoke (air) in your lungs. What you need to rid yourself of will be carried out with it when you exhale. Mentally fill the smoke with anything you need to rid yourself of. Exhale slowly and gently, and be extremely focused on the flame. Try to exhale with enough control to not extinguish the flame, but also to see the smoke collide with the tip of the flame, as if it is burning the smoke and all it carries away. At the end of your exhale, if the candle is still lit, blow it out.

June Full Moon (Strawberry, Lovers', Mead, Honey, Rose)

Intention: To connect with your higher self or higher power for a moment of restful peace to rest and recharge under a summer full moon.

Bong water: Bergamot for peace.

Crystal: Rose quartz for peace and compassion for yourself.

Blend: Chamomile and lavender for peace. Motherwort and rose for compassion, nurturing, peace, and self-love.

Process: Use a space where you can sit or lie down comfortably on a blanket, preferably outside under the full moon. Set up this space with your prepared supplies: bong with infused water (if using), herbal blend, and smoking or tea supplies.

When you are prepared and in place, ritualistically consume your blend and cannabis in a meaningful and mindful manner. Lie down on the ground and say:

> *Moon above me, full and round,*
> *As I lie here on the ground,*
> *Shine your light down on me,*
> *Bless me with peace,*
> *This is my plea.*

Allow the magic time to take place. (If you are using edibles, take them ahead of time to give them a chance to activate in your system.)

Stare at the moon and allow your mind to open. Close your eyes and let your mind drift to a happy place where you feel safe and free. Connect with the energies of the moon and feel peace wash over you. The moon relaxes, refreshes, and recharges you. Spend as much time here as you wish, adding more THC as desired.

July New Moon

Intention: Use the dark of the moon to increase your psychic abilities or other form of divination for more accurate and detailed readings.

Bong water: Use new moon water with an amethyst and moonstone for divination, and a quartz for amplifying.

Crystals: Amethyst and moonstone for divination. Quartz for amplifying your energy.

Blend: *Calea zacatechichi* for insight from the spirit world to guide and assist you. Mugwort for divination and visions.

Process: Use a space where you can sit comfortably and meditate. Set up this space with your prepared supplies: bong with infused water (if using), herbal blend, smoking or tea supplies, and the following:

- Black candle
- Lighter
- Your favorite form of divination (This includes usage of the clair senses.)

When you are prepared and in place, ritualistically consume your blend and cannabis in a meaningful and mindful manner.

Light your black candle and follow the energy waves of the flame. Let it help carry you to a meditative state as your weed takes effect. (If you are using edibles, take them ahead of time to give them a chance to activate in your system.)

Allow yourself to connect to your higher self, higher power, or another spirit entity you choose to work with. Ask for their guidance and their vision in the working you are undertaking. Perform your working, reading, or session as appropriate for your divination method.

July Full Moon (Buck, Hay, Wort, Thunder)

Intention: Utilize the power of the full moon to open yourself to messages from Spirit. If you work with a specific goddess, you will want to focus on her specific energy. Draw down the moon for a message from the divine feminine.

Bong water: Peppermint for cleansing, protection, and boosting your psychic intuition.

Crystals: Amethyst and moonstone for spiritual awareness and opening yourself to messages from deity or Spirit.

Blend: Mugwort and damiana to aid in receiving psychic and intuitive messages.

Process: Use a space where you can sit comfortably and meditate. Set up this space with your prepared supplies: bong with infused water (if using), herbal blend, and smoking or tea supplies.

When you are prepared and in place, ritualistically consume your blend and cannabis in a meaningful and mindful manner. Position yourself for meditation and allow the magic time to take place. (If you are using edibles, take them ahead of time to give them a chance to activate in your system.)

Visualize yourself in your own universal safe space. Invite your image of the divine feminine, a higher power, or Spirit to join with you. What message is there for you? What questions do you have? What answers do you find?

August New Moon

Intention: Remove blockages to creativity. Refresh and let go; get ready to start with a fresh slate. Challenge yourself: What can you produce by the full moon? If possible, do this outside with a blanket on the ground. Otherwise, lie on the floor inside.

Bong water: Clove for cleansing and increasing mental focus.

Crystals: Two quartzes for cleansing.

Blend: Hyssop to remove stagnant energies. Tulsi for restorative energies.

Process: Use a space where you can lie comfortably on the ground. Set up this space with your prepared supplies: bong with infused water (if using), herbal blend, smoking or tea supplies, two quartz crystals (one to hold in each hand), blanket, and pillow. If you work with the chakras, add corresponding stones to your chakra centers. Make your space comfortable so your mind doesn't drift toward anything being physically uncomfortable and you can clearly focus where needed.

When you are prepared and in place, ritualistically consume your blend and cannabis in a meaningful and mindful manner. Position yourself for meditation and allow the magic time to take place. (If you are using edibles, take them ahead of time to give them a chance to activate in your system.)

Lie down on the ground, hands at each side holding a quartz crystal. Meditate on clearing yourself of any negative energy, any blockages, any ick plugging up your creativity. Visualize energy coming from the ground, traveling into the quartz and then moving throughout your body, cleansing as it goes. The energy from the ground that came into the left crystal migrates throughout the body to end at the right palm, where the quartz directs the energy back into the earth to be grounded and neutralized. The same happens with the other side; the right quartz draws energy from the ground, sends it throughout the body to end at the crystal in the left hand, and then directs it back into the ground.

Visualize this pattern repeatedly happening, cleaning, cleansing, and charging you. Focus on the project you will undertake between now and the full moon (this could also be a step or two from a larger project or a timeline section). What do you need to accomplish? Visualize your project growing and becoming more successful with the waxing of the moon. As the moon grows fuller, your project grows closer to fruition.

Keep your crystals in a place where they will be a reminder to also do the mundane work to achieve your goal by the full moon.

August Full Moon (Sturgeon, Corn, Barley)

Intention: Tap into the creativity of the full moon with energy-raising music.

Bong water: Wormwood to increase creativity.

Crystals: Carnelian for creativity. Quartz for amplifying your magic.

Blend: Mugwort and sakae naa leaf for creativity. Use a sativa or sativa-dominant hybrid to help work up energy for this fun full moon.

Process: Use a space (outside if possible) where you can safely set up your prepared supplies: bong with infused water (if using), herbal blend, and smoking or tea supplies. Place them in a safe place so you are able to move around without bumping into them. Choose music you associate with raising energy and be sure to have plenty of it on hand.

Don't just take one hit and dance or move to one song; a half hour to an hour is ideal. Some songs can be slower and just clapped along with. The key here is to distract your mind while you raise energy. Move what you can move and distract yourself with the energy of the music. Let yourself get lost, and while you raise this energy, only focus on raising the energy. Let it build and release several times. Don't focus on any specific problem or issue; only send out a request to the universe for creative answers or ideas. Often when we don't think about something, the answer comes to us unexpectedly. Open yourself to any possibilities. If you focus on one issue, you may miss the presentation of a solution or an idea for something else.

Open your mind and your energy to receive all positive solutions and possibilities. You may discover what you are searching for when you least expect it.

September New Moon

Intention: Removing blockages that hinder thankfulness or generosity.

Bong water: White sage to connect to higher self and increase self-awareness.

Crystals: Amethyst for spiritual work. Quartz for cleansing. Obsidian to absorb negative energy.

Blend: Motherwort provides calmness while working with difficult emotions and supports self-love and healing from emotional wounds. Rose for nourishing your soul. Thyme for healing your soul.

Process: Use a space where you can sit comfortably and meditate. Set up this space with your prepared supplies: bong with infused water (if using), herbal blend, and smoking or tea supplies.

When you are prepared and in place, ritualistically consume your blend and cannabis in a meaningful and mindful manner. Position yourself for meditation and allow the magic time to take place. (If you are using edibles, take them ahead of time to give them a chance to activate in your system.)

Connect with your higher self or power. Think about a time when you know you could have been either more thankful or more generous in a situation. We come across these situations daily, whether it's being more generous with our time, money, intentions, patience, love, etc., the list goes on. We often miss thankfulness or gratitude when we have become accustomed to certain behaviors, relationships, or even material possessions. When we are unable to express these feelings, it is usually for a reason. Listen to what your higher self has to say about where your generosity and thankfulness are lacking and what guidance is offered to remedy any situations.

September Full Moon (Corn, Harvest, Wine, Singing)

Intention: Use the full moon to honor and celebrate your own abundance and prosperity. Celebrate what you have accomplished this year. Whether you feel you have accomplished only a little or a great deal, all your accomplishments deserve recognition. Honor yourself for what you have achieved.

Bong water: Catnip for bliss.

Crystals: Green aventurine to honor prosperity. Rose quartz for nurturing compassion.

Blend: Motherwort to support expressing gratitude. Lemon balm for bliss. Hops to honor abundance.

Process: Use a space where you can sit comfortably and meditate. Set up this space with your prepared supplies: bong with infused water (if using), herbal blend, smoking or tea supplies, your journal or Book of Shadows (depending on where you document specific information), and a writing instrument.

When you are prepared and in place, ritualistically consume your blend and cannabis in a meaningful and mindful manner. Position yourself for meditation and allow the magic time to take place. (If you are using edibles, take them ahead of time to give them a chance to activate in your system.)

Meditate on what you achieved. What have you harvested? Big or small, think over your accomplishments and allow yourself to feel pride in all of them. When ready, document these achievements where you find it most appropriate. When you need a reminder in the future of what you have achieved or overcome, you know where to find it.

October New Moon

Intention: Honor the darkness with shadow work and listen to your ancestors to break and heal generational trauma.

Bong water: Cloves to honor the darkness.

Crystal: Obsidian for protection.

Blend: Motherwort to provide calmness while working with difficult emotions. White sage to connect to your higher consciousness and increase self-awareness. Hyssop for expelling negative energies.

Process: Use a space where you can sit comfortably and meditate. Set up this space with your prepared supplies: bong with infused water (if using), herbal blend, and smoking or tea supplies.

When you are prepared and in place, ritualistically consume your blend and cannabis in a meaningful and mindful manner. Position yourself for meditation and allow the magic time to take place. (If you are using edibles, take them ahead of time to give them a chance to activate in your system.)

Open yourself to listen to messages from your ancestors. What do they tell you needs healing? When we stop generational trauma, we heal ourselves and our ancestors. What messages do you have for your ancestors? What traumas have your worked to heal for yourself and for them? Listen for their guidance on where to turn your attention next.

October Full Moon (Blood, Harvest, Hunter's)

Intention: To meet and communicate with the departed at the veil.

Bong water: Mugwort to aid in spirit communication.

Crystals: Moonstone for full moon divination. Amethyst for divination and spiritual work. Obsidian for protection and spirit communication. Quartz for protection.

Blend: Mugwort, *Calea zacatechichi*, mullein, wormwood, wild lettuce, and blue lotus to help you commune with the spirit world.

Process: Use a space where you can sit comfortably and work. Set up this space with your prepared supplies: bong with infused water (if using), herbal blend, and smoking or tea supplies. Anything you need for the type of spirit communication you generally practice should also be prepared. If you have a specific spirit you would like to contact, having a picture or an item that belonged to them may help you connect to their energy.

When you are prepared and in place, ritualistically consume your blend and cannabis in a meaningful and mindful manner. Position yourself for meditation and allow the magic time to take place. (If you are using edibles, take them ahead of time to give them a chance to activate in your system.) Say:

> *On this night of the full moon,*
> *I call the spirits to commune.*
> *Come to me, if thou are able,*
> *Come and meet me at the veil.*

Open your mind to all possibilities and conduct your spirit communication session.

November New Moon

Intention: Use the darkness of the moon and winter for inner shadow workings. It is time to eliminate what needs to be removed from your life, followed by healing and rest.

Bong water: Rose for healing heart wounds, nourishing your soul, and inner strength.

Crystals: Amethyst for spiritual work. Obsidian to absorb negativity. Rose quartz for self-love and nurturing.

Blend: Motherwort for coping with difficult emotions, nurturing love, peace, and self-love. Jasmine to relieve anxiety and promote restful sleep. Rose for healing heart wounds, inner strength, and nourishing your soul. Hops for peace and rest. Blue lotus flower for sleep. Sacred lotus and lemon balm for restorative rest.

Process: Use a space where you can sit or lie down comfortably to meditate. Set up this space with your prepared supplies: bong with infused water (if using), herbal blend, and smoking or tea supplies.

When you are prepared and in place, ritualistically consume your blend and cannabis in a meaningful and mindful manner. Position yourself for meditation and allow the magic time to take place. (If you are using edibles, take them ahead of time to give them a chance to activate in your system.)

Connect with your higher self or higher power. If you are currently working through a shadow, this will be your focus.

If not, listen to the objectivity of your higher self or power. What do you need to tackle next? Give yourself love and support as you begin this next step of your journey.

November Full Moon (Beaver, Snow, Dark, Fog, Mad)

Intention: To aid in communication with others and yourself.

Bong water: White sage to increase your self-awareness and effect on others.

Crystals: Moonstone to amplify the full moon energy. Citrine to ease communications. Rose quartz for nurturing and communications.

Blend: Motherwort to support openness. Hops for peace. Tulsi for achieving and maintaining balance, healing, calmness, and reducing stress.

Process: Use a space where you can sit comfortably and meditate. Set up this space with your prepared supplies: bong with infused water (if using), herbal blend, smoking or tea supplies, a spell-size yellow candle, and a lighter.

When you are prepared and in place, ritualistically consume your blend and cannabis in a meaningful and mindful manner. Position yourself for meditation and say:

> *As the moon is full above,*
> *Find my heart full of love.*

Help me to see what needs to be seen,
Guide me to understand what it all means.

Allow the magic time to take place. (If you are using edibles, take them ahead of time to give them a chance to activate in your system.)

Connect with your higher self or power and ask for guidance on how you can better communicate with yourself and others. Listen for your answers and practice following through on the given advice.

December New Moon

Intention: Using the darkness of the moon and winter for healing and rest.

Bong water: Rose for healing heart wounds, nourishing your soul, and inner strength.

Crystals: Amethyst for spiritual work. Rose quartz for nurturing self-love.

Blend: Motherwort for coping with difficult emotions, nurturing love, peace, and self-love. Jasmine to relieve anxiety and promote restful sleep. Rose for healing heart wounds, inner strength, and nourishing your soul. Hops for peace and rest. Blue lotus flower for sleep. Sacred lotus and lemon balm for restorative rest.

Process: Use a space where you can sit or lie down comfortably and meditate. Make it extra cozy for this working, especially if you live in a climate where the "dead of winter" is truly felt. Think about warmth and comfort when setting up your area. Include a spot for your prepared supplies: bong with infused water (if using), herbal blend, and smoking or tea supplies.

When you are prepared and in place, ritualistically consume your blend and cannabis in a meaningful and mindful manner. Position yourself for meditation and allow the magic time to take place. (If you are using edibles, take them ahead of time to give them a chance to activate in your system.)

It is the last new moon of the calendar year. It is a long, dark night, perfectly designed for rest. You have worked hard throughout the year. Acknowledge your trials, tribulations, celebrations, and achievements. You have earned this night of comfort, of warmth, of soothing and rest. Give yourself a hug, relax, and rest.

December Full Moon (Cold, Oak, Moon of Long Lights)

Intention: Let the power of the last full moon of the year draw away from you what you need to release before a peaceful rest.

Bong water: Motherwort to support openness and releasing emotional burdens.

Crystals: Moonstone to amplify the power of the moon. Quartz to boost power. Amethyst for spiritual work.

Blend: Damiana and sacred lotus for their emotionally uplifting qualities. Jasmine for elevating your mood and providing restful sleep. Passionflower for restful sleep.

Process: Use a space where you can sit or lie down comfortably and meditate. Set up this space with your prepared supplies: bong with infused water (if using), herbal blend, and smoking or tea supplies. You may want to do this in bed to drift off to sleep without having to move to a different location.

When you are prepared and in place, ritualistically consume your blend and cannabis in a meaningful and mindful manner. Position yourself for meditation and allow the magic time to take place. (If you are using edibles, take them ahead of time to give them a chance to activate in your system.)

Focus on: What baggage do you not want to carry into the new year with you? What weight do you need lifted from your shoulders? What burden does your heart carry? Now is the time to let these things go. Release these things from your heart and mind. While you may not forget, their hold on you is gone. As the moon wanes, they will fade further and further from your mind, their grip lessening and lessening each day. Wrap yourself in a cozy hug and know that your rest ahead is well deserved.

Blue Moon

A *monthly blue moon* is the second full moon in a calendar month and occurs every few years.

Intention: Recognize and celebrate your accomplishments.

Bong water: Peppermint for its energetic focus.

Crystal: Moonstone to amplify full moon magic.

Blend: Rose for happiness and sacred lotus for its mood-elevating, magic-boosting, relaxing, and euphoric-feeling qualities.

Process: Use a space where you can sit comfortably and work. Set up this space with your prepared supplies: bong with infused water (if using), herbal blend, smoking or tea supplies, and your journal and writing instrument. Choose upbeat, celebratory music to accompany you, a small gift for yourself, or even a special treat. (Or all three if you wish!)

When you are prepared and in place, ritualistically consume your blend and cannabis in a meaningful and mindful manner. Position yourself for meditation and allow the magic time to take place. (If you are using edibles, take them ahead of time to give them a chance to activate in your system.)

Think back over the past couple of years about all the things you have accomplished. What stands out the most to you now? What were your most important accomplishments? How did they affect you? What did you accomplish that no one else knows about? Document your answers in your journal.

Celebrate with dance, a gift, or special treat for yourself, and feel proud of your efforts.

Black Moon

A *black moon* is the second new moon in a calendar month.

Intention: Use this clean slate to set a significant goal to achieve before the next full moon.

Bong water: Sacred lotus for its magic-boosting ability.

Crystal: Clear quartz as an amplifier.

Blend: Sakae naa leaf for stimulating and creative energies. Mugwort to encourage your goal to completion and to boost your creativity. Chamomile to help your goals manifest.

Process: Use a space where you can sit comfortably and meditate. Set up this space with your prepared supplies: bong with infused water (if using), herbal blend, smoking or tea supplies, a black candle, a lighter, a small piece of paper and a safe way to burn it (you may move outside to do this if necessary), and a writing instrument.

When you are prepared and in place, light the candle and consume your blend and cannabis in a meaningful and mindful manner. Position yourself for meditation and allow the magic time to take place. (If you are using edibles, take them ahead of time to give them a chance to activate in your system.)

Meditate on what you want to manifest into your life by the full moon. Make it something significant that you can also put a mundane effort toward. Write a manifestation statement as if your goal is already complete.

Use the black candle to light the piece of paper, sending your manifestation into the universe. Continue to meditate on your goal as you wish.

Lunar Eclipse

Intention: Use the power of the lunar eclipse to reveal hidden issues, skills, or talents. This may be emotional and draining, depending on what is brought to light, but it will also be revolutionary.

Bong water: White sage to connect with your higher power and for self-awareness.

Crystal: Clear quartz for clarity.

Blend: California poppy for calmness. White sage to increase your self-awareness, support your meditative state, and help you connect to your higher consciousness. Blue vervain to calm and quiet your mind from distractions. Mugwort to aid in meditation and clear visions.

Process: Use a space where you can sit comfortably and meditate. Set up this space with your prepared supplies: bong with infused water (if using), herbal blend, smoking or tea supplies.

When you are prepared and in place, ritualistically consume your blend and cannabis in a meaningful and mindful manner. Say:

> *While the moon is hidden from view,*
> *We know its light will again come through.*
> *With the emergence of the moon's light,*
> *Reveal to me what's hidden from sight.*

Position yourself for meditation and allow the magic time to take place. (If you are using edibles, take them ahead of time to give them a chance to activate in your system.) Connect to your higher self or power and listen for what is revealed.

Chapter 4
SOLAR RITUALS

Here are some rituals to celebrate the solar events of the year.

Vernal Equinox

The beginning of spring is here with the vernal equinox. Honor the balance today brings. Pick a time of balance to begin this working: sunrise, sunset, noon, 2:22, 4:44, 10:10, 12:12, 1:11, or 11:11.

Smoke your weed blended in a balanced ratio with tulsi for emotional, inner, mental, physical, and spiritual balance, or prepare a tulsi tea and consume your cannabis in a different form. Chant:

> *The darkness ends where the light begins,*
> *Bringing balance on this day.*

When the dark returns and the light is gone,
The balance remains the same.

Meditate and listen to a message from your higher self. Where do you need to find better balance in your life?

Summer Solstice

The summer solstice is when the sun hits its peak; it is the day with the most amount of daylight and the least amount of darkness.

Blend wormwood with your weed in equal amounts (or drink as tea) and sprinkle a few petals from a dandelion blossom on top of it.

Get high outside today. (Hopefully, it's sunny!) Close your eyes and let the sun kiss your face. Imagine yourself soaking in the energy and power from the sun. Let it recharge and revitalize you.

Autumnal Equinox

The balance of light and dark is back, but from now until spring, the darkness wins.

Blend together equal amounts of mullein and chamomile, and then combine with your weed or drink as tea.

Get high and meditate on how this change feels for you. How does the increasing darkness affect you? What do you enjoy about the dark half of the year? What struggles do you face? How do you work to balance yourself and your life through the dark half?

Sunflower seeds represent the sun before it begins losing power. If you enjoy them, snack on them today.

Winter Solstice

The winter solstice is the longest night of the year and the shortest day. It is the epitome of the saying, "It is darkest before dawn." Ancient people understood that surviving through the darkness meant bright, better days ahead. This sentiment still holds true.

Blend together equal amounts of rose, St. John's wort, and mullein to blend with your weed in a one-to-one ratio to smoke or infuse as a tea.

This longest night, get high and meditate on the obstacles you have overcome this year. What darkness did you struggle through to find the light? Honor yourself for the battles against the darkness you have fought and won.

Solar Eclipse

Even if an eclipse isn't completely visible from your location on earth, you can still use this energy. The eclipse happens whether you are an eyewitness to it or not. The energy is here on earth; you need only to access it.

Because a solar eclipse is when the moon passes between the earth and the sun, causing darkness to reemerge during daylight, moon water made from the eclipse holds a specific energy of revealing shadows and illuminating darkness.

Blend equal amounts of peppermint and sweet woodruff, grind together, and then blend in a one-to-one ratio with your weed to smoke, or make it into a tea.

Get into a meditative position and say:

> *The power of the eclipse works to reveal,*
> *The darkness inside that needs to heal.*
> *Hidden shadows brought into the light,*
> *Show me my journey when day turns to night.*

Meditate on what shadow or darkness Spirit wants to reveal to you.

Your Birthday

It's your birthday, so be sure to gift yourself a special treat. Try a new product or strain today. Evaluate your thoughts and experience with it.

Meditate today on your journey through life so far and the role cannabis and your Craft have each played. Journal about your meditation.

Chapter 5
SABBATS RITUALS

Celebrate the Wheel of the Year weed-witch style.

Imbolg

Imbolg is when the earth and the goddess begin their awakening from their winter rest. Awaken yourself and your desires with this working.

Blend: Combine your weed with lavender or consume your THC in a different format while drinking lavender tea.

Simmer pot: You will need a sliced lemon with ¼ cup of lavender buds. You may also use a diffuser with a couple drops of lavender and lemon essential oils.

Process: Set up your simmer pot or diffuser to charge your environment with energies of gentle awakening. Chant:

In this time, in this place,
I slip into a liminal space.
Awaken the earth,
And my desires,
Awaken the goddess,
And creative fires.

Meditate on the awakening of Mother Earth and the awakening of the goddess. How do you envision these two events? What do they mean to you? Meditate on what goals you want to accomplish this year. What will you awaken in yourself? Journal about your experience.

Ostara

It is the beginning of spring; winter's rest is over. It is time for plant life to begin its growing season. Wildlife begin bearing their young. The natural world increases productive and fertile energies.

Blend: Combine your weed with lemon balm and chamomile or consume your THC in a different format while drinking lavender tea.

Process: Smoke your blend or consume your tea. Chant:

This beginning of spring, fresh with new life,
I turn my mind to creating and set aside any strife.
Today is for new beginnings;

I create and set goals for me.
This day I plant the seeds of rebirth,
With my magic,
Blessed be.

Meditate on what seeds you want to plant in your life. What do you want to give birth to in your life?

Journal a list of goals you want to accomplish this year. Include details and update as necessary.

Beltane

Beltane is ripe with the blessings of fertility and productivity. Life is bursting forth as flowers bloom, leaves burst from their buds, animals give birth, and the once-dormant grasses and other plant life have awakened and now reach for the sun. Honor and celebrate fertility and the essence of all life today.

Simmer pot: This simmer pot may be sipped after using it to create the desired atmosphere. It is even better chilled, especially if it is a warm day. For each cup of water, add 1 cup apple juice, 1 sliced apple (remove seeds), and 2 tablespoons mint. This mix sets a fertile, rich atmosphere and makes a cooling fruity refreshment.

Blend: Equal amounts catnip, lemon balm, and blue vervain. Grind together with either a hybrid or a blend of indica and sativa in a fifty-fifty mix, or drink it as tea.

Smoke your blend, drink your tea, and drink your cooled apple mint beverage. Say:

On this day I plant the seeds,
The goals from Ostara I propagate.
Bring to life what I desire,
To nurture, flourish, and cultivate.
Beltane energy in the air,
I conceive what I will grow,
Invent my future, devise my plans,
Let the energy flow.

Put on some music, dance, and focus on giving life to the things you want to manifest in your life.

Midsummer

It is the longest day of the year, it's the beginning of summer, and the goddess is pregnant with the god. The natural world is ripe with an abundance of energy from all living things at the peak of the active season. The energies of growth are in abundance. Life thrives.

Simmer pot: Add lavender, rose petals, a sliced lemon, and a vanilla bean or a splash of extract to the water to simmer and create an atmosphere of bright, positive energy.

Blend: Equal amounts lavender, rose, mugwort, damiana, and wild lettuce. Grind together in a one-to-one ratio with your weed, or drink it as a tea. Say:

> *I honor the goddess and the life she carries,*
> *The abundance of energy and essences vary.*
> *The power of the sun strong and bright.*
> *The longest day and the shortest night.*
> *I pay homage to the life all around me.*
> *At one with the universe. Blessed be.*

Meditate on your role and place in the universe. What are you growing to contribute to the world around you? Journal about your experience.

Lughnasadh

Honor the abundance of the first harvest festival with an offering to your deities or to Mother Earth.

Go outside to a place where you can get high and make an offering. Sit on the ground if you can. Share some of your cannabis with the earth by sprinkling it on the ground. Say:

> *I honor my [deities or higher power] on this day of light,*
> *The first harvest gathered, celebrate it in rite,*
> *With gratitude of abundance, I give this offering.*
> *I sprinkle this cannabis for workings and offerings.*

Meditate on the abundance in your life. What have you harvested? Where have you grown? Journal about your responses. Make a list of your accomplishments.

Mabon

Mabon is the celebration of the second harvest, also referred to as Pagan Thanksgiving. Make today all about giving thanks for the blessings you have and are.

Simmer pot: Create a simmer pot with 1 teaspoon each of parsley, sage, rosemary, and thyme per 1 quart of water.

This simmer pot not only has a rich, earthy scent, but you can also use it as a base for a Thanksgiving soup. To take this pathway, add bouillon to your water, or use broth instead. Chop up your choice of compatible veggies, and if you wish, add meat or tofu. Salt and pepper for both taste and protection. For a heartier soup, add rice, stuffing bread cubes, or other grains. Cook on a low simmer, adding more water as needed.

Whether you make it into soup or not, when you stir the pot, say:

Sacrifices made honored and cherished.
My magic, my soul, my energy replenished.

If you eat this as a soup, repeat this before your meal.

Blend: Add a sprinkle of thyme to the top of your weed.

Meditate on your own thankfulness and the sacrifices others have made not only for you personally but for you as a generation. Think about what others gave up before you were even born to give you the life you have today.

Samhain

Samhain is the third and final harvest of the year. With the thinning of the veil, tonight is perfect for spirit communication. Begin by setting the mood for a night of crossing the veil to communicate with your ancient ancestors or dearly departed.

Simmer pot: This simmer pot of spiced cider is threefold. It smells wonderful, it creates a protective atmosphere conducive to meeting at the gates of the otherworld, and it tastes divine. Simmer cider with apple chunks (remove seeds), cinnamon, and clove to your taste.

Blend: Equal amounts of sacred lotus petals, wormwood, and dandelion leaf. Grind together and either blend in a one-to-one ratio with your weed, or drink it as tea.

Create an apple bong. Do an internet search for instructions to see where exactly to carve out your apple to turn it into a pipe. It's not difficult but may require a little patience to line your holes up correctly.

When you are fully prepped, smoke your blend (or consume in another manner with tea) and sip your spiced cider. Meditate to calm and open your mind. Count backward from one hundred. You are ready to perform your preferred method of divination.

Yule

Yule is the shortest day and longest night of the year. It is when the goddess gives birth to the god and the sun is reborn. Honor and celebrate this day with the following working.

Simmer pot: This simmer pot is also a warm and bright drink, comfy and cozy for the long, dark night, with a bright note to promise the coming light. Add a quart of apple cider to your pot. Slice one orange and one lemon into rounds. Sprinkle in cinnamon and clove to your taste. Simmer on low for twenty minutes to disperse its energy into the air, then pour yourself a mug to sip.

Blend: Lavender, mugwort, blue vervain, mullein. Grind together and combine with your weed in a one-to-one ratio, or drink as a tea and consume your cannabis in another form.

Smoke your blend or drink your tea, and then sip the warmed cider.

Relax in a comfortable position, close your eyes, and let the magic take place. Contemplate what life was like for people on this night one hundred years ago. What type of home would they have had? How did they stay warm? How did they cope with darkness? Go back another one hundred years. How did the people two hundred years ago face the longest night? Continue to think back in hundred-year jumps. Go back as far as you can. Recognize and appreciate the struggles you do not have to face. Journal about your experience.

Chapter 6
THE THIRTEEN WAYS
OF THE WEED WITCH

To round out the 420 spells, rituals, and techniques for this book, here are thirteen ways to embrace being a weed witch.

BONG WATER RELEASE SPELL

Bong water is stale, gross, stinky, and sometimes downright slimy if it's been too long between changings. It's the ick we need to remove in order to have a fresh, clean start. Do this spell before you are ready to clean your bong. You want it dirty for this working.

Smoke your weed in your bong and settle into a meditative state of mind. What do you need to release? What do you need to cleanse from your system? Difficult day at work? Problems seem to pile up all at once? Big things or little things, whatever it is that is bugging you, focus on it now.

Remove the bowl from your bong and gently blow into the mouthpiece while concentrating on what you want to cleanse yourself of. Blow it into the bong. Release what you need to. Empty your bong water and clean your bong.

PUFF PUFF PASS

This spell to release and move on has several uses but is also ideal for ending a relationship. It is best done in the evening during a waning moon.

You will need:

- Spell-size black candle
- Spell-size purple candle
- Lighter
- Moonstone-charged weed
- Clove water in bong
- Writing instrument
- Small piece of paper
- Fireproof container or other safe way to burn the paper.

- **Smoking blend:** Equal amounts of blue vervain, lavender, mugwort, rose

Light the candles in front of you about a foot apart from one another. Smoke your blend, or consume as a tea and consume your cannabis in a different form.

Place the paper in between you and the candles. Write out what (or whom) you need to release. No explanation; keep it brief and to the point.

Take a hit and blow it over the paper, thinking, "I release you." (You may also waft smoke from cannabis incense.) Take a second hit and blow the smoke over the paper again, thinking, "Goodbye." You may say these aloud if you wish.

Crumple up the paper, place it in the fireproof container, and set it on fire with the black candle. Allow it to burn completely and dispose of the ashes.

Meditate on your new future. Give yourself loving kindness if needed.

SPELL FOR NURTURING SELF-CARE

It is important to learn and know when to give magic a break and take care of yourself mundanely.

Smoke a blend (or make tea) from equal amounts of lavender, rose, and sacred lotus flower. Combine this with your weed in a one-to-one ratio.

Do something *you* find comforting. Take a bubble bath, wear comfy socks or footie pajamas, read a book, sit by a fire, watch your favorite movie. Shut off your magic and nurture yourself.

SPELL OF REMEMBRANCE

Some days you need a break from work and a reminder of how far you have come, how you have grown and changed, and what you have overcome and accomplished. Today, take that break.

Light some incense (frankincense or myrrh if available) and then a green candle.

Smoke a blend of sacred lotus petals, mullein, and wormwood (in equal amounts), combined with your weed in a fifty-fifty blend, or drink it as tea. If you like, snack on raspberries to represent remembrance.

Read through your journal, either choosing dates at random or looking for specific influential events or challenges. Remind yourself of your journey so far. Today's work is only to appreciate how far you have come.

SPELL TO BOOST SELF-ESTEEM

Use this spell for a quick self-esteem boost fueled by cannabis.

Smoke a blend of jasmine buds ground together with your cannabis in a fifty-fifty mix, or consume your THC in a different form while you drink a cup of jasmine tea. Get yourself pleasantly high. A blend that rates "giggly" is perfect for this spell.

Sit in front of a mirror with a clear quartz crystal either placed in front of you or held in your hand. Stare into the mirror at the person you see. Smile at them. Really smile. As your reflection smiles back at you, feel the tug to smile more authentically. The person in the mirror will smile more authentically back at you. Play off your own smile. Laugh if you want. When do you see or feel the smile hit your eyes? Know you can give yourself this boost of endorphins whenever you desire.

MANIFESTATION SPELL

Most spellwork is some type of manifestation. We want to bring things into our lives. We want opportunities to appear or to be drawn to us in some manner. We manifest what we desire. What do you want to manifest into your life?

Charge your weed with amethyst and blue apatite.

Incense: Myrrh, patchouli, or sandalwood

Blend: Blue vervain, chamomile, lavender, and rose in equal amounts to use in a tea or blend with your weed in a one-to-one ratio. As you grind and blend your herbs together, focus on what it is you want to manifest.

Light your incense and smoke your blend, or consume it as a tea and take your THC in a different form. Meditate on what you want to manifest. Produce a clear statement focusing on one thing as specifically as you can, but also don't be greedy. Be reasonable. Write out your manifestation statement.

Blow your smoke (or cannabis incense) across the paper. Say:

> *My goals and wishes I define,*
> *What I desire, I make mine.*
> *I petition the universe, my hopes, and needs,*
> *Send what I manifest, my magic succeeds.*

Blow smoke across the paper again.

Go outside and safely light the paper on fire, allowing it to burn completely, releasing your desire into the universe.

SPELL TO AWAKEN AND ACT

This working can be done alone with an intrapersonal intention or as a group with the intention of a community awakening.

Decorate your altar or area with red, yellow, and orange candles. Charge your weed or other cannabis products with red agate, red jasper, and sunstone. Add these stones to your altar or working area.

Blend lemon balm and ginseng in a fifty-fifty mix and drink as a tea or blend with your cannabis in a one-to-one ration to smoke.

Consume your blend or tea and light your candles. Build and release energy with the following chant while focusing on your intention:

> *Awake! Awake!*
> *See what is true!*
> *Awake! Awake!*
> *It's up to you!*
> *Awake! Awake!*
> *Time to engage!*
> *Awake! Awake!*
> *Dawn a new age!*
> *Awake! Awake!*

[My or our] change is strong!
Awake! Awake!
Power raised in song!

Dance to build and release even more energy!

SPELL JAR TO SOOTHE,
CONTROL, OR DIFFUSE ANGER

Similar to a stress ball, when you feel anger or frustration getting the best of you, this spell jar can help you cleanse and rechannel your energy.

You will need:

- Glass jar with lid or corked vial
- Moss agate chips
- Bloodstone chips
- Blue vervain (dried)
- Chamomile (dried)
- Lavender (dried)
- Wormwood (dried)
- Black sealing wax
- Yellow sealing wax
- Purple sealing wax

Smoke your weed (or use another consumption method, allowing time for edibles to take effect).

Place each ingredient into your chosen jar (or mix them in a bowl and then transfer them to your jar), focusing on each one's energy along with your intention. Visualize a protective bubble being created around you as you build and bless your jar.

As you work with each ingredient, say:

I call upon the energies of [ingredient name],
Guide me to calm.

Take a hit (or deep, centered, intention-filled breath if you do not smoke or vape) and use your exhalation to gently blow your hopes and objectives into your jar.

Close the top of the jar and cover it with melted sealing wax, first the black, then yellow, and finish with purple, allowing each color to show. When finished, say:

I am calm.
I am at peace.
Let the good energy flow.
I am okay.
I am relaxed.
I let my anger go.

Carry your jar or vial with you or put it in your car, on your desk at work, or any place where you feel you may need its calming energies. Anytime you need its magic, hold on to it and recite the incantation above.

CBD SPELL TO PROTECT YOUR PET

THC isn't good for animals, but CBD definitely is! Like us, our pets also contain a cannabinoid system, which can benefit from the addition of a CBD supplement. CBD helps your pet's systems reach and maintain homeostasis for better health.

CBD is available for pets through treats and oil to dispense with a dropper. Whether you give your pet a daily dose or an occasional boost, when you do so, add in some magical energy with focused intention and say:

> *With my love, I give this dose,*
> *To protect and keep safe,*
> *The [pet's name] I love most!*

SPELL JAR TO RESTORE BALANCE

Feeling off-kilter? Restore your balance with this spell jar, which incorporates a well-known symbol for balance: the scales of justice.

You will need:

- Small jar with lid or corked vial
- Basil (dried)
- Blue vervain (dried)
- Meadowsweet (dried)
- Mullein (dried)
- Sweet woodruff (dried)
- Justice tarot card image small enough to fit into jar or vial
- Brown sealing wax
- Gray sealing wax
- Green sealing wax

Smoke your weed (or use another consumption method, allowing time for edibles to take effect).

Place each ingredient into your chosen jar (or mix them in a bowl and then transfer them to your jar), focusing on each one's energy along with your intention. Make sure you leave enough room for your image to sit or lie on top of your herbs before sealing the container.

As you work with each ingredient, say:

> *I call upon the energies of [ingredient name],*
> *Guide me in restoring balance to my life.*

Take a hit (or deep, centered, intention-filled breath if you do not smoke or vape) and use your exhalation to gently blow your hopes and objectives into your jar.

Close the top of the jar and cover it with the melted sealing wax, first the brown, then the gray, then the green, allowing all colors to be seen.

To activate your jar, say:

When I feel off and out of whack,
Guide me to get my balance back.

Sit in meditation while holding your jar when you need its power.

COPING WITH CHALLENGES SPELL

Frustrated with a challenging situation and not sure where to turn? Let this spell be your guide in the next steps you take.

Charge your weed with quartz to help you gain clarity over the situation you are facing.

Blend together equal amounts of blue vervain and peppermint, then grind together with your weed in a one-to-one ratio or steep to drink as tea. Focus on the challenge you are dealing with and what type of assistance you need. Do you need aid in brainstorming solutions? Or perhaps aid in accepting what is out of your control? Focus on what it is you need.

Consume your weed, get into a comfortable position, and say:

> *To the universe I ask this request,*
> *Send me what you deem best.*

Meditate and listen for the guidance you seek.

COPING WITH CHANGE SPELL JAR

Change isn't easy, even when it's for the best. When it's not a change for good, it's often more difficult to cope with and accept. This spell jar is designed to give you support to help you deal with changes, whether good or bad.

You will need:

- Small jar with lid or corked vial
- Crushed walnut shells
- Myrrh
- Dandelion (fluff if available)
- Turquoise chips
- Peppermint (dried)
- Sweet basil (dried)
- Sweet woodruff (dried)
- Violets (dried)

- Paper (optional)
- Writing instrument (optional)
- Black sealing wax
- Blue sealing wax
- Green sealing wax
- Yellow sealing wax

Smoke your weed (or use another consumption method, allowing time for edibles to take effect).

Place each ingredient into your chosen jar (or mix them in a bowl and then transfer them to your jar), focusing on each one's energy along with your intention. Visualize a protective bubble being created around you as you build and bless your jar.

As you work with each ingredient, say:

I call upon the energies of [ingredient name],
Support me when I have need of you.

If you are dealing with a specific change, write it on a piece of paper and place it in the jar.

Take a hit (or deep, centered, intention-filled breath if you do not smoke or vape) and use your exhalation to gently blow your hopes and objectives into your jar.

Close the top of the jar and cover it with the melted sealing wax; begin with the black, then blue, green, and finally yellow, allowing some of each color to show. When finished, say:

> *When change comes my way,*
> *Guide my heart and mind from fray.*
> *Give me strength to accept what I must,*
> *Grant me the will to adjust.*

Carry your jar or vial with you or place it in a prominent place in your home. It can also be placed next to your bed while you sleep. This is especially helpful if the change you are dealing with triggers insomnia, nightmares, or other sleep-related issues.

SPELL FOR ACCEPTING ENDINGS

Every beginning has an ending, whether we want it to or not. Sometimes we need help accepting when something or someone's role in our life has ended. This spell will aid you in accepting an ending.

Charge your weed with obsidian.

Blend equal amounts of St. John's wort and wormwood to either drink as tea or combine with your weed in a fifty-fifty ratio. As you blend and grind, focus on the ending you are having difficulties with.

Think *comfort* as you prepare your setting for this working. Consider your clothing, seating, and lighting for maximum coziness. Add in a scent that makes you feel safe and warm. Surround yourself with blankets and pillows if you wish.

Eating tends to make us feel better, so prepare a snack or small meal from your favorite comfort foods along with a warming, soothing drink.

Create a safe, warm, comforting space with everything you need at hand. Smoke your blend or drink tea and situate yourself into a comfortable position. Say:

> *All things end,*
> *Nothing stays forever, including me.*
> *I seek compassion in my grief.*
> *I seek acceptance for this ending.*

Repeat this as often as you need. Give yourself compassion. Give yourself love. Hug yourself. Cry. Release pain, fear, or guilt associated with the ending. Feed and replenish yourself as needed. Let everything out and give yourself the comfort you need.

CONCLUSION

I want to thank you not only for joining me on this specific journey but for all the fun, learning, and interactive lessons along the way, right from my first cannabis book, *Wake, Bake & Meditate: Take Your Spiritual Practice to a Higher Level with Cannabis.*

Cannabis has changed my life for the better, allowing me to live a relatively pain-free life, where my dozen medical conditions have all gone into remission.

From medical to magical, cannabis has not only saved me, but it has also benefitted both my daily and my spiritual lives. I wish you the same results and success!